THE
MEDIEVAL CONTRIBUTION
TO POLITICAL THOUGHT

THOMAS AQUINAS
MARSILIUS OF PADUA
RICHARD HOOKER

THE
MEDIEVAL CONTRIBUTION
TO POLITICAL THOUGHT

THOMAS AQUINAS
MARSILIUS OF PADUA
RICHARD HOOKER

BY

ALEXANDER PASSERIN·D'ENTRÈVES

D.PHIL., PROFESSOR OF PHILOSOPHY OF LAW
IN THE UNIVERSITY OF PAVIA

THE HUMANITIES PRESS
New York 1959

First Published in 1939 by Oxford University Press

Reprinted 1959 by The Humanities Press
by special arrangement with
Oxford University Press

Printed in U.S.A. by
NOBLE OFFSET PRINTERS, INC.
NEW YORK 3, N. Y.

PREFACE

THE lectures printed in the present volume were delivered in the University of Oxford during the Summer term, 1938. Notwithstanding the obvious defects of lectures appearing in book form, I have preferred to preserve their original character, both for sentimental reasons and because it is no part of their purpose to present a complete narrative of the development of medieval political thought.

The argument of the first four lectures mainly corresponds to that of my Italian book, *La filosofia politica medioevale*, published in 1934. The material for lectures V and VI was brought together in England during the years 1926–9, when I was awarded a travelling fellowship on the Rockefeller Foundation. Part of the argument I submitted as a doctoral dissertation on Hooker in 1932. A further account both of the sources I have used and of several questions which I have been unable fully to develop in the lectures can be found in my book, *Riccardo Hooker* (1932).

My indebtedness to contemporary thinkers I have tried to record in the text, but I should like to acknowledge particularly the influence of my Balliol years, and the encouragement which I received from teachers and fellow students in England. I owe an immense debt of gratitude to Dr. A. J. Carlyle, who assisted my work from the beginning; to Mr. A. D. Lindsay for many stimulating discussions; to Professor R. H. Tawney for his penetrating criticism; to Mr. B. H. Sumner and to Mr. R. N. Carew Hunt for their appreciation and friendship. I should like to express my grateful thanks to the University authorities and to the Master and Fellows of Balliol for arranging these lectures, and to Professor F. M. Powicke for all that he has done on behalf of their publication. I am greatly obliged to Miss Margaret Carlyle for revising my English, and to Mr. R. W. Southern for his invaluable help in making my argument more consistent with English usage and ways of thought.

August 1938. A. P. D'E.

CONTENTS

INTRODUCTORY NOTE

By F. M. POWICKE

MANY years ago a philosopher told me that he had been reading Maitland's translation of Gierke on medieval political thought. He expressed delight and astonishment in the discovery that people in the Middle Ages were interested in such matters; and he added: 'I found there attempts to face all the big problems which have been bothering me.' On the other hand, a history tutor complained to me, a little while ago, that he found great difficulty in helping his pupils to read Locke intelligently, because they did not relate his thought to anything. My friend said, indeed, with pardonable exaggeration: 'It is not only that they don't see why Locke should refer to the Scriptures; they don't know what the Scriptures are.'

The six lectures printed in this little book cover in part the same ground and they deal in the same kind of way with medieval political thought as Professor d'Entrèves's two books on medieval political philosophy and on Hooker; but they were given in English by an Oxford man with particular regard to the needs of an Oxford audience, whose acquaintance with the history of political thought is generally confined to selections from the writings of Aristotle, Hobbes, Locke, and Rousseau. A systematic survey of medieval thought, with its vast and perplexing literature, would be quite out of place in a book of this kind, primarily intended for readers who have little or no acquaintance with the history of the West between the age of St. Augustine and the age of Bodin and Hooker. Professor d'Entrèves has, very rightly, concentrated attention upon the great problems of law and obligation—problems which now perplex thoughtful men and women in the world as they have rarely been perplexed before—in the light of the teaching of three strongly marked and strongly contrasted thinkers, St. Thomas Aquinas, Marsilius of Padua, and Richard Hooker. He emphatically repudiates the view that this thought can be appreciated out of its setting, but he asserts, with equal emphasis, that what medieval thinkers had to say about such matters as the nature of political obligation and the relations between the meaning of law and the objects of political association was a positive contribution to later thought. We cannot understand the ways in which Aristotle has influenced thought, or in which Hobbes and Locke and Rousseau approached the political issues and impulses of their times, if we do not know anything about the incessant effort made by men in the Middle Ages to explain *their* political environment. And Professor d'Entrèves would go farther and assert that this body of thought, as transmitted by Hooker and others, has had and still may have a healthy and even crucial influence upon the lives of men.

Professor d'Entrèves, in the first instance, compiled a select, but long, bibliography, which will, I hope, be printed some time; but he felt that this was hardly suitable, and might deter the readers for whom his book is especially intended. We have accordingly added, at the end of the volume, only a brief selection of titles of books and papers.

I

INTRODUCTORY

IT is difficult, if not impossible, to start working on
the history of political theory without immediately en-
countering the difficulty of making clear what exactly is
the subject which we have undertaken, and how it should
be dealt with. Apparently such a difficulty does not occur
in other branches of historical research, or at least it is not
so obvious. The general historian, unless he be especially
gifted for, or interested in philosophical speculation, can
leave problems of 'historiography' to the professional
philosopher. This is not so easy for the historian of
political thought. For what we mean by political thought
is still a matter for discussion, and the study is further
confused by the variety of aims, methods, and assumptions with which it is approached. This lack of agreement
and the uncertainty concerning the relations of political
theory to cognate branches of study such as law, philosophy, psychology, or even biology, can be seen in many
recent discussions. It seems, then, rather perilous to
attempt to retrace the development of a world of thought
whose bounds are so imperfectly known. To content ourselves with the apparently modest aim described by Professor Laski, of gathering, 'in what detail one may, what
men have thought about the state,' does not seem to me
an entirely satisfactory starting-point: for, with all its
modesty and its taking an apparently firm ground in 'real'
as contrasted with 'abstract' purposes, such a definition, if
it is not simply a truism, is grounded on the most question-
able of all premises, namely, the assumption that we know
what we mean by the abstract word 'state'.

By raising some doubts about this last assumption, I not only intend to draw attention to the fact which has many times been pointed out, that the modern meaning of the word 'state' is a comparatively recent acquisition; for not even Machiavelli can be said to have used it in its truly modern sense. My doubts concern the very possibility of bringing under the same heading such different notions as the Greek idea of πόλις or κοινωνία, the Roman conception of *respublica* and *imperium*, the medieval ideal of a *communitas communitatum*, the modern concept of the state. On what ground can we hold together such widely different conceptions and attempt to reconstruct their common lines of development? And even admitting that the continuity of such development might be proved, where do we find the touchstone which enables us to include some ideas as 'political' and to exclude others? We are confronted in the wide field of historical experience with the most varied and complex types of human association. Some of these may appear of only slight importance in relation to the state; others seem to have a most definite political character which would, however, be denied to them, according to our modern idea of politics.

But I do not propose to dwell any further on these difficulties nor to discuss the possibilities of overcoming them by means of a preliminary definition of the proper field of political theory. My purpose is a more modest one, and, if I have raised the question of the method and aims of the history of political theory, I am ready to admit that I have done so, in order to justify my own line of approach to this field of historical research, which will be set out in what follows.

The history of political theory, if it be worthy at all of

a distinct and well-defined place among the many branches of historical research, is, in my opinion, a history of ideas, not a history of political institutions. Of course the two branches of knowledge are closely knit together, and only a lover of paradox would maintain that it is possible to understand, say, the political theory of Aristotle without a fair acquaintance with Greek political life, or that of Machiavelli severed from its close connexion with the conditions in Italy in the sixteenth century. Yet, unless we indulge in the fallacies of a so-called historical materialism, and consider ideas and theories as nothing more than a reflection or 'super-structure' of social and economic phenomena, it is necessary to realize how entirely different our task appears, when, instead of describing the rise and fall of political institutions, we set out to understand the efforts of generation after generation of thinkers to reach a solution to problems which, as philosophical problems, remain essentially unaltered, and necessarily lead us from the proper plane of history into the realm of values.

It is obviously a difficult task to give any clear-cut definition of these problems, but I think that there is one formula which provides us with the best line of approach to, and the fairest approximation of, that primary and lasting problem around which the history of political theory centres. It is the formula which, if I am not mistaken, was drawn up for the first time in this very university by that great thinker, T. H. Green; namely, the term 'political obligation'. Thus, to put it briefly, the history of political theory is to me first and foremost the history of the attempts to solve the problem of political obligation. It may therefore be said of this history, as of all true history, that it is, in Croce's words, contemporary history. Indeed, if there is a field of historical research in which the remark seems to find confirmation, it is in the history of political theory. We need only remember the fine achievements which have been reached precisely by those writers who, like Gierke and Maitland, Figgis and Troeltsch, have turned to this particular branch of research in order to attain a better notion and a firmer grasp of the modern political problem. Of course, some of the criticism which has been directed against the application of this method is justified, and one may recall some pungent remarks of Professor Allen to the effect that 'much of the work that has been done on the history of political thought appears vitiated to some extent by an endeavour to exhibit ideas of the past in relation to something vaguely called "modern thought".' We shall later have some illustrations of this in considering the tendentious interpretations which have been placed on the work of Marsilius. Equally evident are the dangers of certain slogans, of which Professor Powicke has recently endeavoured to rid the study of medieval political thought; for, stimulating though they may be, they easily change from innocent generalizations and modes of interpretations, the use of which is justified by its practical results, into expressions of some particular conviction or bias. The point is, that the acknowledgement of the 'contemporary' character of the history of political thought does not in any way provide a justification for interpreting the ideas and doctrines of the past as a confirmation of our own ideas and doctrines, nor does it free us from the historian's primary and obvious duty of objectivity. What makes such history contemporary history is not the projection of our own petty schemes and preconceptions into the past, but the realization that, however remote those ideas and doctrines may seem, the problem to which they respond remains a constant one and, despite all changes of circumstance, is the problem which still faces us the moment we begin to reflect on and inquire into the foundations of authority and the grounds of political obligation.

Let me then turn to conclusions and set forward what I conceive to be the purpose of these lectures. It is a study of a particular answer which has been given to the problem of political obligation, and of its meaning to us. It is an analysis of a system which we call medieval because it was constructed in its complete outlines by medieval thinkers, but which, as a system of values, obviously calls for consideration not only *sub specie historiae*, but also *sub specie aeterni*. For it remains one of the main possible answers which can be given to that problem which was first set forward as an object of inquiry by the Greeks and has since been one of the most stimulating factors of our western culture: the problem of authority, of obedience, of political obligation.

The idea of contribution, which is emphasized in the title of these lectures, should thus by no means be taken as an excuse 'to arrange the past neatly as a process in which the most significant things are those which are most easily appropriated by the present', but rather as an inducement to realize the necessity of considering medieval political thought, not only as a sum of particular doctrines and rules, but as a system of values. Hence, as implying a particular attitude towards the problem of political obligation, the legacy of medieval political thought ought not to be subjected too closely to the tyranny of dates. Apart from the fact that the terms 'medieval' and 'modern' are purely conventional, to apply them to ideas and doctrines on mere grounds of chronological priority is very misleading.

What matters are the ideas and doctrines in themselves and it is commonplace to say that they are timeless. It is the purpose of these lectures to give evidence of the fact that some fundamental principles and leading ideas, which were given definite form and expression by medieval thinkers, far outstretch in their effects and influence the conventional boundaries which usually limit the medieval period. They have provided the main source of inspiration for several great systems which belong, from a mere chronological standpoint, to more recent times, and which in turn appear as the thread by which medieval political speculation has come to be closely linked to the political consciousness of the modern world.

My own limitations will not permit me to give you a complete analysis of the contribution, but this way of approach should, if my scheme is not too ambitious, provide the ideal link which holds together such widely different thinkers as Aquinas, Marsilius, and Hooker. In my opinion these three names can well be taken to express the main aspects of medieval political thought, for it is in the work of Thomas Aquinas that this living thought finds its highest and complete expression; Marsilius provides us with the best illustration of its sudden and far-reaching crisis; and Hooker affords convincing evidence of the continuity of medieval ideas all through the great spiritual revolutions which we call by the name of the Renaissance and the Reformation. The limits and inadequacy of such a treatment should not be overlooked. It has been pointed out many times, and rightly, that the line of development of political thought does not proceed, as it were, by leaps and bounds from one great thinker to another, and that, if our aim is a fair and adequate reconstruction of that development, we have to take into account not only the complete and constructive systems but also, and even especially, the slow, continuous, and often not fully conscious evolution of political ideas and opinions. It has further been pressed that such ideas and opinions find expression not only in the work of systematic thinkers, but must be retraced to the tacit assumptions or rough intuitions in the general body of thought of a given epoch. It is undoubtedly in the rich *humus* of its literature, its law, its beliefs and fears, that the more developed systems take their roots. But if, to quote one of Professor Laski's happy epigrams (and Professor Laski is certainly one of the most convinced advocates of the study of 'historic environment'), there has been no influential political work that is not, in essence, the autobiography of its time, surely there is some excuse for turning to the great systematic thinkers in order to understand what precisely is the message of their age and its importance as a contribution to the body of political speculation. Let me then try to sum up very briefly what I conceive to be that contribution of which the writers whom I have mentioned should provide an illustration.

The proper substance of that contribution is best realized if we consider separately the several issues which the problem of political obligation raised for the medieval mind. First and foremost among these, if not in actually promoting theoretical developments, certainly in stirring the deepest emotional reactions, we must take into account the religious issue. One of the most commonly received historical interpretations is that which considers the Middle Ages as a great age of Faith. This view has been criticized by recent historians as unduly simplifying the rich and complex variety of medieval life and experience. There remains, however, very much to be said in favour of this old and commonplace opinion, and it is confirmed by the paramount importance which the religious premiss assumes in medieval political thought. Nowhere, in fact, does Troeltsch's well-known thesis, that medieval Christianity represents one of the main forms or 'types' of Christian experience, find a better illustration, for many among the leading political principles of the Middle Ages are in essence nothing else than a particular interpretation of fundamental Christian ideas. In making this statement I do not venture to raise the much discussed question, to what extent, if at all, a properly defined social and political programme is contained or implied in the teaching of the Gospel. This question is, for my present purpose, of secondary importance. The really important fact, of which the endless and tedious adaptation of scriptural texts is but an indication, is surely that the problem of authority and obligation was felt by the medieval mind primarily to involve a religious issue, and urgently to require an answer which should be in accordance with the principles of the Christian faith. It is from this point of view that we can understand, if not actually sympathize with, the extraordinary ingenuity of medieval thinkers in developing, from the bare letter of some well-known texts of the Scriptures, a whole programme of social and political action, which sometimes seems to depart rather far from its original source of inspiration.

One, and perhaps the most discussed of these texts, seemed indeed to provide a direct answer to the problem of political obligation.

'Let every soul be subject unto the higher powers. For there is no power but of God: the powers that be are ordained of God. Whosoever therefore resisteth the power, resisteth the ordinance of God: and they that resist shall receive to themselves damnation. For rulers are not a terror to good works, but to the evil. Wilt thou then not be afraid of the power? do that which is good, and thou shalt have praise of the same: for he is the minister of God to thee for good. But if thou do that which is evil, be afraid; for he beareth not the sword in vain: for he is the minister of God, a revenger to execute wrath upon him that doeth evil. Wherefore ye must needs be subject, not only for wrath, but also for conscience sake.'[1]

The whole history of Christian political theory can well be said to be nothing else than an uninterrupted commentary upon this text. The teaching which it contains marks the radical opposition between the classical and the Christian approach to politics. It implies that political values can no more be conceived or represented as a purely human concern. They involve the deepest religious implications. Obedience has ceased to be a merely political problem; authority has assumed a sacred character. Yet from these basic assumptions very different inferences could be and were, in fact, drawn. The Christian notion of obedience has in time been developed into a doctrine of passive obedience as well as into a theory of the religious duty of resistance; the idea of the sacred character of authority has provided the background both of the divine right of kings and of limited and responsible government. Medieval political thought is deeply involved in these issues. It is thoroughly imbued with the idea that authority and obedience are at bottom not merely a political, but a religious concern. But in their interpretation of this leading Christian idea, medieval writers followed a path of their own, which led to conclusions widely different from those which were reached by older and by more recent Christian interpreters. Far from fostering an unqualified acceptance of the existing order, far from

---

[1] Rom. xiii. 1–6.

providing an excuse or a cloak for the crudest political 'realism', by means of which, as is the case with St. Augustine, the hardships of political life could be explained away if not actually justified as an expression of the will or the wrath of God, the duty of obedience and the sacred character of authority were to medieval writers a potent incitement to action, a tool for fearless criticism of existing institutions, a stimulus to transform them in accordance with the Christian ideal of social and political justice. No doubt this particular attitude was made possible by the particular character of medieval political experience: the experience of a world as it were in the making, and in which the actual christianization of life could seem infinitely more probable than it had been in the ancient world, or was ever to be in the modern. But behind this particular attitude, which certainly deserves to be considered as the result of particular historical circumstances, there lies a contribution to political thought which is of permanent value. The idea that authority, whatever its origin, its forms, or its aspects, has in itself some element that never is and never can be merely human; that therefore the exercise of power is a source less of rights than of duties, and obedience is due less to man than to principles; that it is the subservience to the divine order of justice which alone can legitimate political rule and give it a 'divine' character: such principles, which medieval thinkers contrived to develop from the original sources of Christian experience, have become outstanding landmarks of Christian political thought, and must remain such unless Christianity abdicates all hope of constructive political action and takes refuge in a passive acceptance of the powers that be.

Very much the same remarks can be made with regard

to another passage from the New Testament, which is even more commonly conceived to express a leading principle of Christian politics, and records the words of our Lord: 'Render unto Caesar the things which are Caesar's, and unto God the things that are God's.'[1] Here again we find at the root of the Christian outlook an idea which flatly contradicts the older conception of politics. As the highest attainment of human life, as an embodiment of the ultimate end of the individual, the ancient state, as a great classical scholar once put it, was both a state and a Church. Christianity, although preceded in this path by dissolvent philosophical criticism, marks the definite cleavage between political and ethical values, a cleavage which necessarily leads to an opposition, if not actually to a conflict of allegiances. The true Christian, as the officials of the Roman state very soon experienced, and as all state-officials are sooner or later bound to realize, is a man who does not necessarily refuse obedience, who may even sometimes believe it his duty to practise passive obedience, but who never will rally to a theory and practice of undivided allegiance, nor accept Caesar's word for an ultimate authority. And yet this leading idea has found very different interpretations. In its original context the Christian teaching seems simply to imply a disparagement of the 'things which are Caesar's', and a rendering of them to him as being insignificant in comparison with true Christian values. But medieval Christianity succeeded in developing into a complete programme of social and political relations a doctrine which had perhaps in its origins a purely religious significance. The main outlines of that programme have been described over and over again. I need not remind you of certain very expressive

[1] Matt. xxii. 21.

formulae which have been recently circulated, and have obtained success even beyond the restricted circle of specialized historians. The 'Gelasian principle', the notion of the *respublica christiana*, of the 'one society' with its 'two hierarchies' or 'two departments', have become commonplaces of every description of medieval as contrasted with modern political thought and experience. I have already pointed out what I conceive to be the merits and the dangers of such generalizations. I cannot see any reason for not using them, provided that we never forget that they are, and were to those who drew them up— Gierke, Sohm, Bernheim, Figgis—a mere canon of interpretation, a means of bringing into prominence and, as it were, of re-creating the deep and fundamental motives underlying a complex trend of historical development.

If we put it this way, we shall not be surprised if particular systems and thinkers do not always fit perfectly well into these schemes. No doubt the idea of the *respublica christiana* is simply an approximation; but it is an approximation which is of great help in visualizing the main points in which medieval political theorists, even though of very different opinions, are fundamentally at one. It is the clearest summary of the particular manner in which medieval Christianity interpreted and gave practical expression to the distinction between the things which are Caesar's and those that are God's. It is the key to a proper understanding of the medieval notions of *regnum* and *sacerdotium*, of their mutual relations and of the complex symbolism which they inspired. And thus, last but not least, it is a warning against the danger of taking our modern notions of church and state too much for granted and forgetting the inexhaustible variety of interpretations which the Christian ideal has produced.

Although, however, the medieval approach to the
problem of political obligation appears to be primarily
inspired by religious motives, it would be a great mistake
to infer from this fact that medieval thinkers conceived
of no other answer to the problem itself except that which
could be drawn from scriptural sources. Had this been
the case, there would probably have been no legacy of
medieval political thought worthy of the name, for the
problem of politics would have been entirely shifted on to
the plane of religious duty, which obviously allows of little
discussion. It is one of the striking features of medieval
Christianity that its reliance upon dogmatic premises did
not, as has been the case with other forms of Christian
experience, finally lead to the disparagement or suppres-
sion of rational inquiry. The problem of political obligation was thus felt to involve not only a religious, but a
purely human issue: an issue, that is, which required to
be faced not only by appealing to faith, but by resorting to
criticism, in order to explain the existence of political
institutions and their value in relation to the nature and
destiny of man. It is for this purpose that medieval
thought endeavoured to construct a theory of politics not
only upon a religious, but upon a philosophical and legal
basis.

Medieval political theorists, in their philosophical construction of the state, combined a variety of different
material, and it is perhaps appropriate to say that their
originality lies not so much in the contribution of new
ideas as in the recreation of old ones into a definite system
which only on careful examination discloses itself as a
patient and elaborate patchwork. These doctrines and
principles, as Dr. Carlyle has conclusively shown, fall into
two main categories and derive from the two main currents

of thought which in turn influenced the development of medieval political theory: the inheritance of Stoic and early Christian ideas on one side, the revival of Aristotelian philosophy on the other.

It is no business of mine to discuss the momentous problem of the fusion of Stoic and Christian ideas into a body of doctrine which dominated European thought for a period of over a thousand years. The affinity between Christian thought and certain ideals and principles of Stoicism is perhaps best explained by their having both been developed during that great moral and intellectual upheaval which marked the decline of the classical ideal of the city-state. The new consciousness of individual values and ends which was brought to birth in Stoicism and Christianity has remained a lasting and vital factor in our western civilization. The idea of one universal society, of one universal law of nature, of the fundamental equality of men, inspires the body of thought which leads from Cicero and Seneca to the great Roman lawyers and the Fathers, in whose writings they were transmitted to later ages. These principles allowed, of course, of different interpretations. Thus, as Troeltsch has pointed out, the idea of equality assumed a very different meaning as interpreted by the Stoic and the Christian. But there is one common element in the political philosophy which they inspired: the idea, namely, that only a great and momentous change could account for the contrast between the present political and social institutions of man and his original freedom and equality. Then again, the Stoic and the Christian could meet in their acceptance of a conception which had appeared already in older philosophies, and had soon developed into a potent weapon for the criticism of existing institutions, the conception of a contrast between nature and convention, between φύσις and νόμος. But in their explanation of the state as a system of organized force, the Christian writers could lay the greatest possible stress upon an idea which, though not unknown to the Stoic, only found its direct confirmation in dogma and biblical teaching: the idea of human corruption and sinfulness. Thus Christian political philosophers, recognizing the conventional character of social and political institutions, were not necessarily led to attribute to them a voluntary or contractual origin. They stressed the character of the state as a conventional but necessary institution, as a divinely appointed *poena et remedium peccati*.

Here again we are met by one of those formulae which are very often used and misused by the student. I have no doubt that this particular one has been greatly overrated, and is in fact completely misinterpreted when taken to imply a purely negative attitude to the state, an unqualified assertion of its sinful origin. This is certainly not in general the standpoint of medieval, and probably not even of earlier Christian writers, despite the opposite view held by some well-known authorities, and despite some definite expressions of this negative attitude produced in the heat of medieval controversy. The formula, however, deserves to be kept in mind as containing the essence of Christian political thought down to the days of the discovery of a new and very different theory of politics: the view that the state was the necessary and divinely appointed instrument of the *pax terrena*. At bottom it was a pessimistic formula, which made it impossible to give the state any positive value as a condition of human perfection, and which was therefore in profound contradiction with the general outlook of late medieval Christianity on the problems of social and political life. It is this later attitude, so different from the passive resignation of primitive Christianity, which perhaps affords the best explanation of the success of Aristotelian political ideas, when, along with the great body of Aristotelian philosophy, they began to be re-discovered and circulated in the thirteenth century. Here was a clear and definite doctrine of the state not as a conventional, but as a natural institution, which allowed of a rational explanation and gave to social and political institutions the very highest value as being necessary for the fulfilment of human capacities and ends. Starting from this assumption, it was possible to overcome the old idea of a contrast between human nature and political conditions, and, more important still, of a contrast between the ends of the individual and those of the state. I shall try in the following lectures to illustrate some aspects of the complex developments which these ideas provoked in medieval political theory. Aristotelian schemes and doctrines made it possible for such thinkers as Thomas Aquinas to draw up the catholic programme of a thorough christianization of life, which did not leave out of its frame the intricate world of social and political relations, but attributed to them a positive value for the enrichment of human nature. Yet, on the other hand, it was this return of the classical and pagan ideal of the state which was the leaven of a very rapid transformation, leading to the final destruction of medieval political thought and to a new conception of the state, wholly incompatible with Christian premisses. In the opposition and conflict of these different motives lies one of the most dramatic aspects of the legacy of medieval political thought.

While attempting to provide a rational, that is, a philosophical explanation of politics, medieval theorists attributed a capital importance to the legal basis of authority. This particular aspect of medieval political theory has always impressed and sometimes also puzzled the modern student. Gierke has well expressed the importance of the idea of law in medieval political speculation:

'Medieval doctrine, while it was truly medieval, never surrendered the thought that law is by its origin of equal rank with the state and does not depend upon the state for its existence. To base the state upon some ground of law, to make it the outcome of a legal act, the medieval publicist felt himself absolutely bound. Also his doctrine was permeated by the conviction that the state stood charged with a mission to realize the idea of law: an idea which was given to man before the establishment of any earthly power, and which no such power could destroy. It was never doubtful that the highest might, were it spiritual or were it temporal, was confined by truly legal limitations.'

I have endeavoured in the following pages to analyse some part of the contribution of medieval political thought which can be referred to this fundamental idea, and to suggest the reasons for its lasting influence upon later developments. It has become the fashion to speak after the example of Figgis of the *damnosa hereditas* of certain factors which seem more directly responsible for the decline of the medieval conception, and foremost among these it is usual to consider the influence of Roman law.

No doubt the revival of Roman law was a decisive factor in the transformation of European political thought, and its importance might well be compared to that of the revival of Aristotelianism in the sphere of philosophical speculation. It worked havoc with the archaic conception of custom, which was the starting-point of medieval theories of law, and thus provided the basis for that legal

4547 D

conception of sovereignty which is usually, though not quite accurately, associated with that of absolutism. But it is important to remember that its influence could not but foster a belief in natural law as the basis of all legal order. It was, in fact, this idea of natural law which helped to justify the restoration of the Roman system, on account of its very reasonableness and universal value, as the law of an international civilization. And it is through the vehicle of natural law that the old idea of the independence of law as against the state was transmitted to later ages. It is on this basis that the recognition of a legal order superior to the state has found momentous development even in more recent days, as the modern theory of international law sufficiently proves. The real and far-reaching challenge to the medieval idea of the priority of law as the embodiment of justice comes from a different side. We shall see its beginnings in Marsilius, but we find its complete development only in Machiavelli and Hegel. It is the doctrine that the state itself, however (as it undoubtedly is in Marsilius) democratically ordered, and however (as again in Marsilius) limited in its executive power, is the embodiment of justice, and thus the source of law. Against this stands the traditional notion of the law of nature as the ultimate source of all legal values. The new idea shakes the whole structure of medieval thought and shifts the religious, the philosophical, and the legal bases of political obligation; and we are left to wonder which of the two opposing views, still openly defying one another, will in the end prevail.

II

THOMAS AQUINAS

THOMAS OF AQUINO (1225–74) is not only the greatest representative of Scholastic philosophy and the most constructive and systematic thinker of the Middle Ages. He is also and foremost the typical exponent of what a recent historian has called the catholic mind. To him we owe an elaborate programme of that thorough christianization of human life which inspired the medieval ideal, and was soon to be celebrated in the immortal poem of Dante. In the formidable apparatus of his work all the aspects and issues of that programme are discussed, all the means of historical, scientific, and philosophical knowledge of the time are used to secure its realization. It is sometimes lamented that St. Thomas should not have left us a clear and definite account of his own political theory; but it is fairly easy to reconstruct the main outlines of that theory from the several indications which are contained in his work, provided that we never forget the general frame into which they fit, and from which they draw their significance. Such indications are to be found in almost all of St. Thomas's works, from the Commentary on the *Sentences* of Peter Lombard to the great *Summae*, from the Commentaries on the *Ethics* and *Politics* of Aristotle to the little treatise *De Regimine Principum*. The latter writings would at first sight appear the most appropriate source for the knowledge of Thomistic political theory; but the use which we can make of them is hampered by the doubts which have been raised as to the authenticity of some of their parts, and by the very limitation of the problems which are dealt with in them. However, the particular aspects of the doctrine matter much less than the fundamental problem around which the whole of Aquinas's political thought can be said to centre, and this in turn can only be understood in relation to the main body of Thomistic philosophy. This fundamental problem is that of the nature and value of political experience.

I have endeavoured in the preceding lecture to illustrate the different issues which this problem raised to the medieval mind. As in all other fields of philosophical speculation, the rediscovery of Aristotelian philosophy in the thirteenth century had a profound and sudden effect in the field of political theory. The classical conception of the state, which was contained in the writings of Aristotle, was in its very essence opposed to the body of ideas and doctrines which had constituted the traditional starting-point of Christian political thought. Dr. Carlyle, in his *History of Mediaeval Political Theory in the West*, has given us some striking examples of the tenacity with which these older ideas held ground down to the very eve of the recovery of Aristotelian political theory. He has provided evidence of their presence in the works of Albert the Great, the teacher of St. Thomas Aquinas, by whom the grafting of Aristotelianism on to the body of Christian thought was begun; a task which his famous pupil was to complete. The proper meaning and the historical significance of the political theory of Thomas Aquinas thus appear strictly correlative to his great enterprise of reconciling Aristotelianism and Christianity, and to the philosophical, or rather metaphysical premisses which seemed to make that conciliation possible. This metaphysical premiss must be mentioned briefly, for it has a direct bearing upon the essence and meaning of Thomistic political thought. It is the idea of a fundamental harmony between human and religious values, between reason and faith. In giving a clear formulation to this idea, Thomistic philosophy appeared to express the deep and intimate aspiration of medieval Christianity, so different in its attitude towards the world and nature from the diffidence and hostility of the early Christian, and the rigid alternatives which had been stressed by St. Augustine. Human values and truths are not necessarily obliterated by the revelation of higher ones; however modest and low, they deserve to be considered as possible tools for the great task of building up Christian civilization. In St. Thomas's assertion, *gratia non tollit naturam, sed perficit,* there is the recognition of the existence and dignity of a purely 'natural' sphere of rational and ethical values. This essentially 'human' standard of justice is not vitiated by sin nor absorbed in the glare of absolute and divine justice; it is rather the first and necessary step in the long ascent towards the fulfilment of the Christian ideal. This sphere of natural and human values finds its complete expression in the idea of natural law, which thus appears as the proper ground upon which social and political relations can be secured and comprehended.

A complete analysis of the Thomist idea of natural law is out of the question. The best description of its purpose and meaning is perhaps that which has been made many times, of a bridge thrown, as it were, across the gulf which divides man from his divine Creator. In natural law is expressed the dignity and power of man, and thus of his reason, which allows him, alone of created beings, to participate intellectually and actively in the rational order of the universe. This explains the stress which is laid in Thomistic philosophy upon the ideas of reason and order (*ordinatio*), which in turn are developed into a complete

and elaborate philosophy of law. Law itself is conceived
as the expression not so much of the will as of the reason
of the legislator: it is, in St. Thomas's well-known expression, *aliquid rationis*, an *ordinatio rationis*. This definition
itself has momentous theological, as well as legal implications. It has remained ever since as the highest expression
of an 'intellectualistic' as against a 'voluntaristic' theory
of law. It is the key to a proper understanding of that
'rationalistic' bent which is one of the distinctive features
of Thomistic philosophy. Its decisive influence is to be
felt in every aspect of St. Thomas's political theory. But
above all, it explains his attitude towards the problem of
political obligation, and his acceptance of a theory, like that
of Aristotle, which involved a rational explanation of the
state and attributed a positive value to social and political
institutions, as being grounded in the very nature of man.
As Dr. Carlyle has pointed out, St. Thomas did not in
all respects directly and categorically contradict the older
explanation of those institutions as the result of, and divine
remedy for, sin. The idea of sin and of its consequences
remained for him, and could not but remain, a fundamental
dogma of the Christian faith. But, as St. Thomas expressly puts it, sin itself has not invalidated *ipsa principia
naturae*. Its consequences, therefore, only concern the
possibility of man's fulfilling the dictates of the *naturalis
ratio*, not his capacity of attaining to their knowledge: in
other words they do not shatter in the least the existence
of a sphere of purely natural ethical values, and it is in this
sphere that the state and political relations find their *raison
d'être*. It has been rightly remarked that the different
manner of conceiving the necessity and foundation of the
state, before and after St. Thomas, derives from a different conception of human nature: instead of considering

the state as an institution which may well be necessary
and divinely appointed, but only in view of the actual conditions of a corrupted mankind, Thomas Aquinas followed
Aristotle in deriving the idea of the state from the very
nature of man. But here again the idea of natural law, and
the conception of a harmonious correspondence between
the natural and the revealed order which it expressed,
provided a solid ground for further developments. For
the Aristotelian conception, with its insistence upon the
'natural' character of the state and its exaltation of the
state itself as the fulfilment and end of human nature, contained at bottom a challenge to the Christian idea of the
existence of higher and ultimate values, and of the inadequacy of merely human means for their attainment. The
natural order, which comprises and sufficiently justifies
political experience, is for St. Thomas only a condition and
a means for the existence of a higher order, as natural law
is but a part of the eternal law of God. If *gratia non tollit
naturam*, certainly also *natura non tollit gratiam*, and nature
requires to be perfected by grace. Thus the action and
value of the state, as part of the natural order, must be
considered in the general frame of the divine direction of
the world, and is entirely subservient to that direction.
The recognition of the value of political experience is thus
subjected to a very important qualification. But it is this
clear-cut delimitation which made it possible for St.
Thomas to attempt his conciliation of the classical and of
the Christian ideal of the state, and, within these well-
drawn limits, the influence of Aristotelian ideas caused
a deep and thorough-going reconstruction of medieval
political thought.

Political institutions are, then, according to St. Thomas,
an aspect or part of 'natural' morality. As such they can

be considered and justified on a purely human plane, independently of religious values, which do not alter the
natural order of which the state is a necessary expression.
This implies that even a non-Christian or pagan state is
endowed with a positive value, as against St. Augustine's
conception of the pagan state as the embodiment of the
civitas terrena and the work of sin. This idea is expressed
in a well-known passage of the *Summa Theologica* :[1]

'It must be granted that government and authority are derived from
human law, while the distinction between believers and unbelievers
is introduced by divine law. Now the divine law, which is founded
on grace, does not abolish human law, which derives from natural
reason. Hence the distinction between believers and unbelievers,
considered in itself, does not abolish the government and authority of
unbelievers over believers. Such a right of government or authority
can, however, be justly abolished by the decision of the Church:
for unbelievers, on account of their unbelief, deserve to lose their
power over believers, who are become the sons of God. But this the
Church sometimes decrees and sometimes not.'

It is here very clearly stated that political authority has
a value of its own, independent of religious belief; and it
has such value as the expression of a natural and rational
order. The intervention of the spiritual power, of the
Church, may sometimes deprive the non-Christian ruler of
his authority; but such intervention is justified on the ground
of that general mission of control of the Church upon the
temporal sphere which will be examined shortly. It in no

[1] *Summa Theol.* 2a 2ae, q. x, a. 10: 'Considerandum est, quod dominium et
praelatio introducta sunt ex jure humano; distinctio autem fidelium et infidelium
est ex jure divino. Jus autem divinum, quod est ex gratia, non tollit jus humanum,
quod est ex naturali ratione. Ideo distinctio fidelium et infidelium, secundum se
considerata, non tollit dominium et praelationem infidelium supra fideles.
Potest tamen juste per sententiam vel ordinationem Ecclesiae . . . tale jus dominii
vel praelationis tolli: quia infideles merito suae infidelitatis merentur potestatem
amittere super fideles, qui transferuntur in filios Dei. Sed hoc quidem Ecclesia
quandoque facit, quandoque autem non facit.'

way qualifies the statement that political authority is in itself fully justified as an expression of human and natural law. Let us notice once again how the question is referred back to the fundamental principle that grace does not abolish nature: the justification of the state and of political institutions must thus be sought in the very nature of man.

This is precisely the leading idea which St. Thomas derives from Aristotle. Few expressions are repeated so often, every time St. Thomas approaches the problem of politics, as that, *homo naturaliter est animal politicum et sociale (ut Philosophus dicit, ut probatur in I° Politicae,* &c.). I must leave it to better philologists than myself to ascertain whether and up to what point the Thomist expression *animal sociale et politicum* may be said to correspond to the Aristotelian πολιτικὸν ζῷον. But if, as I believe, the Aristotelian notion of the political nature of man, as developed in the first book of *Politics*, somehow includes the notion of a social consciousness, and of the necessity for the state having its deepest roots in social experience —over and against the opposite and Machiavellian conception of the state as a work of art, the creation of a powerful but single will—the Thomist expression can be said to render fairly adequately the more important aspect of the Aristotelian conception of politics.[1] The importance which St. Thomas attributes to that conception is explained by him over and over again. In one place[2] he describes man as subject to a *triplex ordo*, divine law, reason, and political authority: this last is necessary in view of

---

[1] It is interesting to notice that William of Moerbecke, in his latin translation of the *Politics*, translated πολιτικὸν ζῷον *animal civile*, and this expression is maintained by St. Thomas in his Commentary on the *Politics* in William of Moerbecke's translation. But the words *animal sociale et politicum* are constantly used in the *Summa Theologica* and in the several other works relating to politics.

[2] *Summa Theol.* 1a 2ae, q. lxxii, a. 4.

the social and political nature of man, for if indeed man
had been by nature a solitary animal, the order of reason
and that of revealed law would have been sufficient. Hence
the necessity, if man is to attain his proper end and realize
the highest form of life and virtue, of his sharing in
political life, and of his practising the *virtutes politicae*.[1]
It is extremely interesting in this respect to observe
St. Thomas's attitude in his Commentary on the *Politics*
of Aristotle towards the Aristotelian doctrine of the 'monstrous' condition of man deprived or abstracted from
political life. St. Thomas was forced to make an express
reservation in favour of asceticism, in favour of the idea of
a higher degree of perfection to be attained by retiring
from the world rather than by participating in it. But he
did not fail to emphasize the exceptional character of a
life of this kind, and the necessity, for the attainment of
such an ideal, of more than human capacities:[2]

'If any man should be such that he is not a political being by nature,
he is either wicked—as when this happens through the corruption
of human nature—or he is better than man—in that he has a nature
more perfect than that of other men in general, so that he is able to
be sufficient to himself without the society of men, as were John the
Baptist and St. Anthony the hermit.'

The idea of the social and political nature of man leads
to an emphatic assertion of the full and harmonious integration of individual life in the life of the community:[3]

---

[1] *Summa Theol.* 1a 2ae, q. lxi, a. 5.

[2] *Commentary on the Politics*, lib. I, lectio 1: 'Sed si aliquis homo habeat
quod non sit civilis propter naturam, aut nequam est, utpote cum hoc contingit
ex corruptione naturae humanae, aut est melior quam homo, in quantum scilicet
habet naturam perfectiorem aliis hominibus communiter, ita quod per se sibi
possit sufficere absque hominum societate; sicut fuit in Joanne Baptista, et beato
Antonio heremita.

[3] *Summa Theol.* 1a 2ae, q. xcii, a. 1: 'Cum igitur quilibet homo sit pars civitatis, impossibile est quod aliquis homo sit bonus nisi sit bene proportionatus bono
communi.'

'Since therefore each man is a part of the city, it is impossible that any man should be good unless he is well-proportioned to the common good.'

But what is the ultimate meaning of such 'integration'? Does it not imply in some way a belittlement, if not actually a denial of the value of human personality? Does it not lead to a complete absorption of individual life in that of the state? Here lay one of the greatest dangers of the return of the pagan conception of the state, which, as was shown by further development of the Aristotelian influence, menaced the fundamental Christian idea of the supreme value of human personality. If the whole is prior to its parts, if the end of the individual is inferior to that of the community, how can the value of human personality be secured? Does not the state become a sort of Leviathan which devours and annuls the individual? That such views are radically incompatible with the Christian teaching is clear not only to the modern student; it was realized very soon by medieval writers, and it was on this very ground that the charge of heresy was brought against so good a Thomist as Dante. It is therefore of the greatest importance that we should correctly understand and interpret St. Thomas's teaching on this momentous issue. But this is far from being an easy task. According to St. Thomas, the common good is undoubtedly more important than that of the individual: *majus et divinius est bonum multitudinis quam bonum unius*.[1] But what is the real difference between the one and the other? In a passage of the *Summa Theologica*, quoting Aristotle, St. Thomas seems to conceive of a difference in quality:[2]

---

[1] *De Regim. Princ.* I, cap. ix: id. in *Summa Theol.*, 2a 2ae, q. xxxi, a. 3.

[2] *Summa Theol.* 2a 2ae, q. lviii, a. 7: 'Bonum commune civitatis et bonum singulare unius personae non differunt solum secundum multum et paucum, sed secundum formalem differentiam: alia est ratio boni communis et boni singularis,

'The common good of the city and the individual good of each person not only differ as being, the one more, the other less, but they are different in kind. The essence of the common good is different from that of the individual good, as that of the whole differs from that of the part. And hence the Philosopher in the first book of the Politics says that it is wrong to assert that the city and the household and other similar associations differ only in quantity and not in kind.'

The doctrine that the end of the whole is of a different quality from that of the part is a dangerous one, as the Dominican critic of Dante, Guido Vernani, writing in the early fourteenth century,[1] was at pains to demonstrate on the evidence of St. Augustine, St. Thomas, and Aristotle themselves. Yet on the other hand, in the *De Regimine Principum*, resuming the elaborate theory of ends which is expounded in the third book of the *Summa contra Gentiles*, St. Thomas openly acknowledges that the end of the single individual and that of the whole cannot and must not be judged on different standards ('idem autem oportet esse judicium de fine totius multitudinis et unius'), and that in fact the end of the one and of the other are substantially the same ('oportet eundem finem esse multitudinis humanae qui est hominis unius').[2] This must mean that the difference between the end of the individual and that of the whole can only be a difference in quantity, and not in quality; that, in other words, the 'integration' of the individual in the whole must be conceived of as an enlargement and an enrichment of human personality, not as a degradation of the individual to the mere function of a part with no value of its own. Thus the Christian idea

sicut alia est ratio totius et partis. Et ideo Philosophus, in I° Polit. (cap. I), dicit quod "non bene dicunt civitatem et domum et alia hujusmodi differre solum multitudine et paucitate, et non specie".'

[1] *De Potestate Summi Pontificis et de reprobatione Monarchiae compositae a Dante Aligherio*, 1327.

[2] *De Regim. Princ.* I, cap. xiv.

of the value of individual personality appears to be safe-
guarded, and is further reasserted in the conception, which
has been analysed above, that however paramount and
important the state may appear for the fulfilment of human
nature, political life is in its turn but a condition and means
for the attainment of a higher type of perfection. This
again implies that the individual can never be completely
absorbed by the state, that something in him is reserved
for a higher end: 'man is not formed for political fellowship
in his entirety, and in all that he has . . . but all that a man
is, and can do, and has, must be directed to God'.[1] Clearly,
the revival of the classical and pagan ideal of the state
called for very important and substantial qualifications.

And yet, notwithstanding such qualifications, the teaching of Aristotle bore in the political thought of Aquinas
some remarkable fruit. This is well seen in St. Thomas's
treatment of the origin of the state and political institutions. According to Aristotle, the problem of the origin
of the state is entirely independent of that of its rational
justification. The doctrine of the political nature of man
primarily implies the idea that, whatever the earliest conditions of mankind, the political condition is its 'natural'
one. It is therefore quite pointless to argue about the
causes of some supposed change in man, and to seek in
them an explanation and justification of the state and
political institutions. There is no place in such a doctrine
for a contrast between 'nature' and 'convention'. The
influence of this doctrine upon St. Thomas is clearly
apparent in his treatment of the idea of a state of nature or
status innocentiae, which is the object of careful discussion

---

[1] *Summa Theol.* 1a 2ae, q. xxi, a. 4, *ad 3um*: 'Homo non ordinatur ad com-
munitatem politicam secundum se totum, et secundum omnia sua. . . . Sed totum
quod homo est, et quod potest et habet, ordinandum est ad Deum.'

in the first part of the *Summa Theologica*. The whole tradition of Stoic and Christian political philosophy was consonant and dogmatic on this point. The teaching of the
Fathers could leave no doubts on the subject of the
original condition in which mankind had been placed by
God. St. Augustine, in a well-known passage which St.
Thomas does not fail to remember, had stated that God
made the rational man to be the master of other animals,
not of his fellow men, thus showing by visible signs what
is the proper order of nature and what are the consequences of sin.[1] The traditional doctrine of the law of
nature, transmitted in the works of the Roman lawyers and
in Justinian's *Corpus Iuris*, had even more emphatically
asserted the original freedom and equality of all men,
and contrasted the institutions which can be referred to
the *ius naturale* with those, such as property, slavery, and
existing political organization, which are grounded upon
the *ius gentium*. Here again St. Thomas does not directly
and categorically contradict these conceptions. His
answer to the difficulty raised by the contrast of two opposite modes of thought clearly shows his efforts of adaptation and the balance of his mind. It may be scorned as a
typical instance of scholastic *distinguo*, but the distinction
is important and far-reaching in its results. The fundamental equality of human nature, a capital tenet of the
Christian faith, cannot be doubted. But the actual in-
equalities which are inherent in social and political conditions must be carefully assessed. St. Thomas here
distinguished between *subiectio servilis* and *subiectio civilis*.
The first is undoubtedly contrary to nature, and can therefore only be explained as a consequence of sin. But the
latter, the relationship of authority and obedience between

[1] *De Civitate Dei*, xix. 15.

men which is necessary for the attainment of the good of all, in a word, political relationship, is by no means a consequence of sin, for it is founded upon the very nature of man. Such a relationship would therefore no doubt exist even if the *status innocentiae* had been preserved. The reason for this is again that, according to Aristotle, man is a social, and hence a political animal.[1] The combination of the two opposite doctrines is clearly apparent, but it is important that the idea of sin, without being rejected, should be confined to narrow limits, merely to explain some necessary hardships of social and political experience, such as the penal character of laws, or the existence of tyrants. But the idea of sin has no part in the rational justification of the state, and the way is thus clear for the reception of a large part of Aristotelian teaching.

The same balance between opposite doctrines, and the same understanding of the value of Aristotle's ideas, appears in the remaining sections of St. Thomas's political theory. In these he is concerned more directly with practical issues, such as the sources of authority, the duty and limits of obedience, the forms and aspects of government. St. Thomas's views with regard to these several problems have been the object of much, and not always discriminating discussion. The causes of this particular interest lie in the fact that since the acceptance of Aquinas's teaching as representing somehow the official expression and foundation of the teaching of the Catholic Church, it has become of the highest importance to ascertain its proper meaning, and to explain how St. Thomas's authority has been claimed to support widely different attitudes, varying from the maintenance of almost democratic tenets at the time of the Counter-reformation to the almost

[1] *Summa Theol.* 1a, q. xcii, a. 1, and q. xcvi.

unconditional acceptance of absolutism in later days. Our Italian liberals of the period of the *Risorgimento*, such as Bertrando Spaventa, did not fail to point out this apparently inexplicable contradiction. Here again St. Thomas's position can only be understood by distinguishing the different lines of approach which he endeavoured to reconcile.

With regard to the problem of the foundation and sources of authority, it is fairly easy to distinguish the various doctrines which have left their traces on St. Thomas's thought. The idea that the foundation of political power, or to use expressions more consonant with the medieval vocabulary, the source of the authority of the law, lies in the community, is, as Dr. Carlyle has never tired of warning us, one of the chief principles of medieval political thought. It is one to which, as he again has conclusively shown, both the older view of the supremacy of customary law and the revival of Roman conceptions equally contributed. For however different in their premisses and practical implications, they could both be interpreted, and were in fact interpreted, as expressing the idea that the people is the only ultimate source of law and of political authority. But although this idea can undoubtedly be traced in several passages of St. Thomas's works, we are by no means authorized to read into his teaching, as some interpreters have done, an assertion of the idea of popular sovereignty. Although clearly admitting that the proper foundation of law and authority is the will, or at least the consent of the community, St. Thomas nowhere committed himself to anything which may be said to approach even remotely the idea of an 'original' or 'natural' right of the people. Hence the acknowledgement of the human source of authority can be reconciled with the fundamental Christian idea of its divine and sacred character; if 'dominium et praelatio introducta sunt ex iure humano', it is also true that 'non est potestas nisi a Deo'. This distinction and reconciliation assumes in one place[1] the aspect of a typically scholastic distinction between 'form' and 'substance', between the *causa formalis* and the *causa materialis* of authority. The ultimate divine source of all authority (*causa formalis*) does not exclude, but on the contrary requires a determination of its actual human and historical origin (*causa materialis*). But there is a third motive, along with these two traditional ones, whose influence is clearly to be felt in St. Thomas's theory of the foundation of power: it is the Aristotelian idea that, since political relationship is grounded in nature, the real foundation of the *ordo inter homines* must be sought in the different capacities of men, in their 'natural' inequality. Hence the best *ordinatio* of the *humanum regimen* is that which corresponds most closely to that inequality, and respects that *praeeminentia intellectus* which is the real justification of power. This lends to St. Thomas's teaching a much more aristocratic than democratic flavour.[2]

When from the problem of the source of authority we turn to that of obedience, it is obvious that the influence of Aristotelian ideas will not be so clearly visible, for this problem assumed in Christian political theory an importance unknown to the classical world. This is the direct result of the Christian ideas of divided allegiance and of the religious value of obedience. And yet it is of great interest to notice that, according to St. Thomas, the duty of obedience is not only a precept of divine law, directly traceable to the biblical texts which have already

---

[1] *Comm. on the Sent.* II, dist. xliv, q. ii, a. 2.

[2] Cp. *Summa Theol.* 1a, q. xcii, a. 1; q. xcvi, a. 4; and esp. *Summa contra Gent.* III, c. 81.

been quoted, but also a precept of natural law. This precept allows of a rational justification, which is grounded precisely upon the Aristotelian argument of the natural foundation of the political relationship.[1] With regard to the limits of obedience, the detailed analysis of the several issues raised in St. Thomas's careful discussion cannot be attempted here. It is enough to remember the main principle which St. Thomas develops, that, as the duty of obedience to authority is grounded both upon divine and upon natural order, its limits are necessarily fixed by the correspondence of human authority with divine and natural law, that is, with justice. This leading idea is developed in the discussion of the value of human law in the section *De Legibus* of the *Summa Theologica*,[2] and formulated with all possible clearness in the section *De Obedientia*:[3]

'It must be said that a man is so far obliged to obey secular princes, as the order of justice requires; hence if their authority is not just but usurped, or if they command that which is unjust, a subject is not obliged to obey, except, according to the circumstances, to avoid scandal or peril.'

The practical applications of this principle, the determination of the modes and consequences of an eventual refusal of obedience, necessarily lead to a complex casuistry. The most discussed instance is that relating to the possibility of active resistance, which to some interpreters has appeared to imply nothing less than an authorization of tyrannicide: a theory which, as is well known, found

---

[1] *Summa Theol.* 2a 2ae, q. civ, a. 1.

[2] *Ibid.* 1a 2ae, q. xcvi.

[3] *Ibid.* 2a 2ae, q. civ-cv: 'Dicendum, quod principibus secularibus in tantum homo obedire tenetur, in quantum ordo justitiae requirit: et ideo si non habeant justum principatum, sed usurpatum, vel si injusta praecipiant, non tenentur eis subditi obedire, nisi forte per accidens, propter vitandum scandalum vel periculum.'

some famous applications in the hands of Catholic writers
of later days. In my opinion, although St. Thomas's
apparent justification of tyrannicide is accompanied by
important qualifications which practically amount to a
flat disavowal of it, there can be no doubt of his acknowledgement not only of the right, but of the duty of resistance to an unjust power.[1] His teaching on the subject
can thus be said to bear witness to that transformation of
the Christian doctrine of obedience into a doctrine exactly
opposed to the theory of passive obedience held by older
and later Christian political thinkers. I have already
pointed out that this transformation is one of the most
characteristic features of medieval political theory.

We find ourselves again in touch with Aristotelian ideas
when, from the discussion of authority and obedience, we
turn to the determination of the forms and aspects of
political organization and to the definition of the nature
and essence of the *communitas perfecta*, or what we should
call the attributes of the state. The decisive influence of
the Aristotelian definition of the state upon the development of medieval political thought has been vividly
depicted by Gierke. It is evident, he notes, that as soon
as men take this definition in earnest, only some among
the various subordinated and superordinated communities
can be regarded as being states. Thus the revival of the
classical conception of the state helped to destroy the
medieval ideal of a universal community or *imperium
mundi*; and it prepared the way for the modern idea of
the particular and sovereign state. St. Thomas's teaching
affords a striking confirmation of this trend of ideas
which has been described by Gierke. The state, as the

---

[1] Cp. *Comm. on the Sent.* II, dist. xliv, q. ii; *Summa Theol.* 2a 2ae, q. xlii, a. 2;
De Regimine Princ. I, cap. vi.

communitas perfecta, is, according to St. Thomas, of an intrinsically different nature from all other communities. This difference can be inferred from the state's capacity for making laws endowed with a *potestas coactiva*, and its possession of a 'sufficientia ad omnia necessaria vitae', the two Aristotelian attributes of autonomy and autarchy. These requisites are fulfilled by two main types of organization, the *civitas* and the *regnum*, which thus deserve the name of *communitates perfectae*; clearly, the Aristotelian notion of the πόλις undergoes a noteworthy extension. But in its essence, it is the Aristotelian notion of the particular state which bears full sway. There is no open mention, in the whole of St. Thomas's work, of the idea of a universal empire. Many explanations have been given of this curious fact, and they may all contain some part of the truth. But, strange though it is that St. Thomas should have been silent on an issue usually considered as the very backbone of medieval political thought, the causes of this silence are not so important as its implications. Does it imply a complete abandonment of the ideal of a superior unity of mankind, transcending the particularism of single political units and expressing an aspiration for absolute values? This, and this alone, would be a sign that the continuity of medieval thought had undergone a sudden and far-reaching interruption. But this is certainly not the case with St. Thomas. The idea of the fundamental unity of human life, for one thing, undoubtedly inspires the whole of St. Thomas's philosophy of law, with its assertion of the unity and universal value of the supreme principles of justice, from which the several systems of positive law derive their substance and value. The same idea is preserved in the conception of the *corpus mysticum ecclesiae* and of the *unus populus christianus*, which embraces and

unites the widest variety of countries and nations.[1] But
above all it is preserved in the idea of the supreme divine
government of the world, which is the highest expression
of that *principium unitatis*, of that *ordinatio ad unum* which,
as Gierke again pointed out, assumed in medieval eyes the
value of a constituent principle of the universe. Thus
behind or above the manifold human types of life and
political experience there is a fundamental oneness: as
St. Thomas expressly puts it, 'etsi sint multi regentes,
eius (scil. Dei) regimini omnes subduntur'.[2]

When from the definition of the state and its attributes
we turn to consider its organization and structure, we are
confronted with a further confirmation of the tenacity
with which medieval conceptions still hold their ground
in St. Thomas's political theory. The influence of Aristotelian ideas is here practically neutralized, as appears from
the very method with which St. Thomas sets about to
determine the best form of government. This, as is expressly set forth in the second chapter of the *De Regimine
Principum*, must be determined in accordance with the
highest and most abstract metaphysical premises, of
which the lesson of experience can only provide a confirmation. Thus the arguments in favour of monarchy as
the best form of government are mainly of a deductive
character: first and foremost among them is the argument derived from the *principium unitatis*, upon which
Dante was soon to base his abstract deductions in the first
book of the *Monarchia*. Yet, when it comes to defining the
organization of monarchy, and to facing some fundamental issues such as the relation of the ruler to the law, or
the nature of tyranny, the influence of, and the reference

[1] *Summa Theol.* 3a, q. viii, a. 1–4; *Summa contra Gent.* IV, c. 76.
[2] *Summa contra Gent.* III, c. 1.

to, actual historical experience are deep and continuous.
I am afraid that I shall have to omit a complete analysis of
this interesting section of St. Thomas's political theory,
and content myself with a brief summary of what in my
opinion are its more important aspects. With regard to
the problem of tyranny, the teaching of St. Thomas in the
Commentary on the Sentences appears to contain the germ of
a distinction which bore its fruits in later thinkers.[1] This
is the distinction between tyranny *ex parte exercitii* and
tyranny *ex defectu tituli*, of which the important developments in fourteenth- and fifteenth-century Italian political
theory, from Bartolus to Coluccio Salutati, are well known.
With regard to the relation of the prince to the law,
St. Thomas's discussion of the Roman principles 'quod
principi placuit legis habet vigorem' and 'princeps legibus
solutus',[2] is of capital importance for the history of the
influence of Roman legal ideas upon medieval political
thought. I have pointed out in my preceding lecture that
the reconstruction and appreciation of that influence by
the modern historian appears to me to be vitiated by an
undue simplification of its complexity, and by the attri-
bution to it of the largest share of responsibility for the
spread of those 'absolutist' ideas which led to the final dis-
ruption of medieval political theory. An attentive study
of St. Thomas's position should be a safeguard against
such tendentious interpretations. For St. Thomas shows
a thorough understanding of the Roman doctrine of the
superiority of the prince (or of whoever has the function
of making law, which may also belong to the whole multitude) to the law from the point of view of mere legal
experience; that is to say, with regard to positive law. It

[1] *Comm. to the Sent.* II, dist. xliv, q. ii.
[2] *Summa Theol.* 1a 2ae, q. xc, a. 1; q. xcvi, a. 5.

is from the authority of the prince, or, generally speaking, from the *potestas publica*, that law derives its *vis coactiva*, its positive legal value. Hence, with regard to this *vis coactiva*, the *potestas publica* is really *legibus soluta*. This acknowledgement of a principle which, without qualification, is substantially nothing else than the principle of sovereignty, ought to induce reflection in the many who still repeat the old slogan that 'there was no conception of sovereignty in the Middle Ages'. Yet in St. Thomas the principle is at once qualified by the important proviso that, *quantum ad vim directivam*, the prince is no doubt subject to the law, albeit nobody except God can compel him to submit to it. Further, the *voluntas principis* has *vigorem legis* only inasmuch as it is *ratione regulata*. Both the *vis directiva* and the *regula rationis* are indeed nothing else than the expression of that natural and rational order of justice which limits the sovereignty of the particular state.

Moreover, along with this fundamental limitation to the 'absoluteness' of sovereignty, St. Thomas conceives of other possible limitations within the state itself, and is even at pains to show their necessity. This is clear in his theory of the practical organization of political power. The real meaning of St. Thomas's teaching on that point, or rather its bearing upon the actual historical possibilities and problems of his time, have recently been an object of careful inquiry, especially with regard to the curious theory which he expounds about the excellency of a 'mixed constitution'. On this point, the main features of the *regimen mixtum*, which is referred to in the *Summa Theologica*,[1] should be considered in connexion with the discussion as to the most convenient establishment of

---

[1] *Summa Theol.* 1a 2ae, q. xcv, a. 4; q. cv, a. 1.

the *regimen unius* which is found in the first book of the
De Regimine. It is fairly easy to see that the best structure
of a political régime is, according to St. Thomas, some
form of limited monarchy. This limitation implies the
dependence of the prince on the rule of law as the
expression of the will of the community. Political power,
though in essence, and according to the Roman teaching, *legibus solutus*, must be constitutionally limited. The
mutual interaction of opposite doctrines and of the main
issues of medieval political experience are thus clearly
apparent in St. Thomas's teaching, and it is significant
that it was precisely to his authority that, two centuries
later, one of the first theorists of the English constitutional system, Sir John Fortescue, repeatedly referred,
when he defended limited monarchy, not only as the
traditional system inherited of old, but as the best of all
possible forms of government.[1]

Finally, there remains to be examined St. Thomas's
attitude towards the problem of the relation between the
temporal and the spiritual powers. Unfortunately his
thought on this subject is nowhere systematically expounded. As Cardinal Bellarmin was later to complain
on this point, 'de Sancto Thoma quid senserit non est tam
certum'. The clearest account of St. Thomas's position is
contained in the fourteenth chapter of the first book of
the *De Regimine Principum*. It is the doctrine of the necessity of a dual direction in human affairs, of the insufficiency
of the *humanum regimen* and of its integration with the
divinum regimen. This duality is reflected in the *regnum*
and *sacerdotium*. There is no need to point out the traditional character of this doctrine, although, as Grabmann

[1] *De Natura Legis Naturae*, c. xvi, xxvi; *De Laudibus Legum Angliae*, c. ix;
The Governance of England, ch. i.

has remarked, its connexion with the Aristotelian doctrine of ends is undoubtedly a novelty in the development of medieval theory. It is with a view to the full attainment of human ends, which culminate in the *fruitio divina*, that the necessity of the two powers is shown; and although this duality converges into unity in Christ, who is both *rex* and *sacerdos*, in this world the two powers are committed separately, the one to earthly kings, the other to priests, and principally to the Roman pontiff, 'ut a terrenis essent spiritualia distincta'. The different value of these ends necessarily implies a subordination of the one power to the other, of the *regnum* to the *sacerdotium*, and hence it follows that to the *summus sacerdos*, the successor of Peter, the vicar of Christ, the Roman pontiff, 'omnes reges populi Christiani oportet esse subditos'.

However clear and definite in its outlines, this doctrine is far from being free of all ambiguity. Let us remark for one thing that St. Thomas does not conceive of a relation between two different societies, between state and church in any modern sense, but of a distinction of functions (*gubernationes, regimina, ministeria, potestates*). But it is the relationship itself which leaves the field open to un-certainty. To some interpreters, the assertion which is made in the *De Regimine* of the necessary 'subjection' of the temporal rulers to the authority of the Pope, has seemed to imply an unconditional acceptance of that so-called 'theocratic' doctrine which found its celebrated assertion less than half a century later at the hands of Boniface VIII and of his supporters. But such an inter-pretation is, according to the best Thomist authorities, quite inaccurate. It is enough to consider attentively the argument of the *De Regimine Principum*, to convince oneself that the subordination or *subiectio* of the civil to the spiritual power of which St. Thomas speaks, is such only with regard to the end.[1]

The Thomist doctrine of the two powers and of their relationship can thus be taken to express the normal medieval doctrine, and to summarize that particular interpretation which medieval Christianity contrived to give of the fundamental Christian idea, to which I have referred in the introduction. It is a doctrine which must not be confused with later interpretations, which in turn represent other and different developments of the Christian ideal. It can be called a theocratic doctrine, but only in the sense that it admits of the necessary and supreme unity of all power in God. It is a very different doctrine from that which is usually called 'theocratic' and which asserts the actual sovereignty, the *plenitudo potestatis* of the Pope over the world. A reference to this latter idea which, as Professor Scholz has conclusively shown, marks in many ways the end of medieval conceptions proper, can be found in the third book of the *De Regimine Principum*, which is commonly attributed to Ptolemy of Lucca. According to the most authoritative interpreters, the teaching of Aquinas only implies the assertion of an indirect power of spiritual over civil authority, a power of guidance and control, which is a consequence of the superiority in value of the ends to which spiritual rule is directed. But, on the other hand, the fully developed theory of the *potestas indirecta*, the typical doctrine of the post-tridentine Church, is a later development of the Christian ideal, a development

---

[1] Nowhere in this treatise, at least in the parts (book I and first chapters of book II) which can be with certainty attributed to St. Thomas, does St. Thomas contradict the teaching which is contained, though not fully developed, in several passages of the *Summa Theologica*, and which is substantially coherent with the Gelasian doctrine of the distinction and comparative independence of the two great spheres of human life.

of which no doubt the germs are already contained in St. Thomas's teaching, but which represents an adaptation of the catholic doctrine to a social and political condition greatly different from that of the Middle Ages. It implies the definite abandonment of the medieval idea of unity, which had provided the ground for the Gelasian principle and for the notion of the *respublica christiana*, and the recognition of a new problem unknown to the Middle Ages, the modern problem of the relation between church and state.

III

MARSILIUS OF PADUA

THE *Defensor Pacis* of Marsilius of Padua (1324) is a landmark not only in the development of medieval political theory but in the history of political thought as a whole. Such, at least, is the unanimous judgement of modern historians, although they differ considerably in their account of the reasons for this capital importance of Marsilius's work. The boldness and coherence of the doctrines which it contains have deeply impressed the historians of medieval thought, and their enthusiasm, which is reflected in an ever-growing production of essays and studies on Marsilius, is responsible for the spread of an almost legendary reconstruction of his figure, as the forerunner and prophet of modern times. The author of the *Defensor Pacis* has been hailed in turn as the announcer of most, if not of all, the doctrines which were to become the creative forces of the modern era, a precursor of the Reformation, a theorist of popular sovereignty and constitutional systems, a herald of the modern sovereign state: a rather curious, and even incompatible, assortment of doctrines. In more recent times, the students of Marsilius seem to have become more critical. They have warned us against the mistake of reading into his words a modern meaning which was never there. They have endeavoured to study and to value the teaching of the *Defensor* in relation to the political problems and theories current in its time. They have carefully retraced the possible sources of the apparently revolutionary doctrines which are expounded in the famous treatise. Yet, with all this, the enigmatic figure of this fourteenth-century Italian is still far from being cleared of all ambiguity, and the real meaning and value of his work still remains a cause of deep perplexity to the historian. The very fact, as Professor Previté-Orton has remarked, that it should have been necessary to prove that Marsilius was no incredible anachronism, is the best tribute to his anticipation of the future: no one needs to convince us that Dante is not modern. Again, as even the more careful critics are forced to admit, several points, at least, of the programme drawn up in the *Defensor Pacis*, were to be realized in later circumstances, and many of its boldest theories bear a striking similarity to those of the more revolutionary 'doctrinaires' of later days. For my own part, I have already pointed out how hopeless I consider the discussion of such issues, and, indeed, whatever may in the end be the right opinion concerning the 'modernism' of Marsilius, the decisive importance of his position is sufficiently clear even when, instead of considering him in relation to later developments, we approach his work from the point of view of medieval thought. It is here that, if I am not in turn misled by my own preconceptions, the idea of a medieval contribution to political thought can be of some help. For, if we take Thomas Aquinas's great systematization as the expression of one fundamental aspect of that contribution, it may seem fair and adequate to consider Marsilius's theory as its exact counterpart, expressing an entirely different answer to those main problems which it is the merit of medieval political speculation to have raised and transmitted to us. I am of course well aware how abstract and arbitrary such a scheme may appear and undoubtedly is. Let me beg you not to take all this too much for granted, and simply to retain the main idea, which has inspired this short digression, that there are reasons enough for selecting

Marsilius's work to illustrate an aspect of medieval political thought radically different from and opposed to the one which we have analysed in St. Thomas. Thus we can leave aside the exciting question of its 'modernism', difficult though it is to remain entirely neutral when such momentous issues as the value of ideas are involved.

Even though we confine the problem of the interpretation of Marsilius's thought to these well-defined and more moderate limits, it is no easy task to sum up in a short formula the characteristic features of the *Defensor Pacis* as a landmark of medieval political theory. It has been said that its 'novelty' consists in the reversal of the normal approach to the problem, which was fundamental in medieval politics, of the relation between church and state.

'Before the appearance of the *Defensor Pacis*'—writes Professor McIlwain—'all defenders of secular government had been content to take a merely defensive position, which was logically untenable in the face of a clerical attack which claimed that Christendom was a *regnum*, in which the *plenitudo potestatis* of the Pope as "ecclesiastical monarch" was the ultimate and supreme authority over all. The great significance of the *Defensor Pacis* lies in the fact that in it for the first time the secular state claims a practical equality which can only be obtained by a theoretical superiority. By the extremer papalists the state for some time had been treated as a subordinate department of the Church. The *Defensor* is the first book which reverses the process and regards the Church as a department of the state in all matters of earthly concern.'

A description such as this succeeds excellently in throwing light upon the historical background of Marsilius's work. It points out the essentially polemical character of Marsilius's teaching, and makes clear the terms of the polemic, as they had resulted from the formulation of the 'theocratic' programme by the extreme clerical faction of schoolmen and canonists. The reversal of a process implies a recognition of the process. In other words, the position taken up by Marsilius in the *Defensor Pacis*, however novel, presupposes a penetrating transformation in the traditional conception of the dual government of human life, which had dominated medieval thought from Gelasius in the fifth to Aquinas in the thirteenth century. But this description somehow leaves in the shade a different background, far more important for the understanding of Marsilius's doctrines: the background of the general ideal premises which provide the basis of his particular conception of the state and are the source of its lasting value. It is these which determine his particular answer to the problem of political obligation.

It is upon this plane that, in my opinion, we must look for the key to the problem; and it is upon this higher plane in fact that the more recent students have felt it necessary to centre their efforts. But, again, they have produced many formulae in their attempt to illuminate the secret of Marsilius, and all seem to contain some element of truth. I do not think it necessary to discuss the obvious exaggerations, such as those of some Italian Hegelians, who have thought it possible to find in Marsilius the germs of the 'ethical state'. There is much, though, to be said in favour of M. de Lagarde's recent interpretation of Marsilius as one of the highest representatives of the *esprit laïque*; and Professor Previté-Orton has brought important evidence of the striking application of the inductive method in Marsilius as contrasted with the typically deductive method of medieval thinkers. Again, if we look at the bent of his theory of the state, of law, and even of morals, we can well term Marsilius a 'voluntarist', as opposed to

the 'intellectualist' Thomas Aquinas. But at the root
of all such formulae, and as a condition for their proper
use, we must endeavour to see in Marsilius, as we have
seen, though far more coherently expressed, in Thomas
Aquinas, a theory of values, a metaphysical premiss. This
metaphysical premiss is in many points the reverse of the
one which we have analysed in St. Thomas. Where
Thomas Aquinas had proposed to conciliate the spheres
of reason and of faith, the rights of critical inquiry and the
duty of submission to a revealed order, the value of natural
ethics and that of Christian virtue, Marsilius draws a clear-
cut and impassable line of demarcation. This is one of the
points in which the influence of a particular current of
medieval philosophy—Averroism—upon the thought of
Marsilius appears as a decisive factor. I shall have to
return to this question of influences, which, obviously
enough, must be solved not only by internal, but also by
external evidence. It suffices here to note the radical
divergencies between the Thomist and the Marsilian philosophical outlook. The only point which they have in
common is their admiration for Aristotle. But, in opposition to St. Thomas and to Dante, Marsilius does not
believe that a study of *philosophica documenta* might well
agree with the acceptance of religious dogma, and should
somehow constitute the appropriate nourishment of *fides
quaerens intellectum*. This radical opposition between
rational truth and religious convictions has been rightly
compared to the averroistic doctrine of a twofold truth.
He carefully distinguishes and opposes the things 'quae
possunt per humanam certitudinem assignari', such as the
res manifestae per se or the teaching of *aperta* and *sensata
experientia*, to those which 'simplici credulitate absque
ratione tenemus'. His unveiled scepticism works havoc in

the elaborate system of co-ordination between reason and faith, between human and divine authority, which had been built up by the Thomist.

This is the crucial point of Marsilius's position, because it is upon these general premises that Marsilius embarks on his own particular interpretation of the main issues of medieval political thought. From these general premises there flows not only a new method of historical interpretation and inquiry, whose devastating effects are clearly visible in the second part of the *Defensor Pacis*, but an entirely new valuation of Aristotle's teaching with regard to the problems of morals and politics. For St. Thomas, the acceptance of the Aristotelian teaching had been possible on the ground of the supposed harmony between reason and faith, between *natura* and *gratia*. The 'Philosopher' had been granted ultimate authority in the sphere of 'natural' ethics on the assumption that the revealed Christian values (the *ius divinum quod est ex gratia*) had not shattered the natural order (the *ius humanum quod est ex naturali ratione*) of which Aristotle's moral and political philosophy was regarded as the highest expression. Yet on the other hand this natural order had to be fitted in, and adapted to the exigencies of the Christian ideal; and we have seen the complex work of adaptation which hence resulted.

But now the meaning of Aristotle's political theory appeared in a very different light. His teaching could be valued for itself, unhampered by any concession to religious belief. His description of political realities could inspire a free reconstruction of the actual political forces which Marsilius, a citizen of fourteenth-century Italy, saw at work in his own country and age. The Aristotelian method of inquiry, applied to the field of social and political life, was used to subvert all theological preconceptions. The classical and pagan ideal of the state as the highest embodiment of human perfection appeared as truly irreconcilable with the fundamental duality of Christian life, and dealt a severe blow to the traditional idea of the existence of an order of justice prior and superior to the state, as expressed in the body of divine and natural law. It is, in fact, the revival of a new Aristotle, which the prudent schoolmen had contrived to exorcize. And yet at bottom the Marsilian interpretation is no less a distortion and adaptation than that of the Thomist had been. There is not the slightest hesitation on the part of Marsilius when it comes to stitching together Aristotelian motives and typically medieval ideas, and the stitches are generally clearly visible. More serious still, Marsilius appears in many points radically to misinterpret the very essence of Aristotle's teaching. His reconstruction and interpretation of Aristotelian doctrines is very often merely external and mechanical. All this leads to a great complexity of problems, which have not yet been entirely cleared up by the students of Marsilian thought. I do not propose, for my own part, to exhaust these difficult questions, but simply to direct your attention, as I did in the case of Aquinas, to the main outlines of a theory which raised such new and momentous issues in the history of political thought.

The purpose and aims of the *Defensor Pacis*, together with the explanation of its title, are set forward by Marsilius in the introductory chapter of his work. Curiously enough, the starting-point of our radical innovator is nothing else than a conception which is a traditional and leading motive of medieval inspiration from St. Augustine to Dante: the idea of *pax*. The supreme achievement of human fellowship is for Marsilius, as for the most

orthodox medieval writers, the attainment of peace.
Peace is not only an ideal, it is the condition of a well-
ordered *civile regimen*. Hence it is that the Philosopher
had taken such pains to describe and to analyse the causes
which might imperil it; but to these causes a new one,
of which Aristotle and the older philosophers had been
ignorant, had to be added. Marsilius describes it as[1]

'a unique and hidden cause of discord which has long troubled
and continues to trouble the Roman Empire; one which is
contagious, equally bent on insinuating itself into all other civil
bodies and kingdoms and has already greedily attacked many of
them.'

This menace to the peace, this ultimate cause of all the
evils which had befallen Italy, was the Papacy, with its ill-
fated pretension to the *plenitudo potestatis*, with its false and
wicked doctrine of the functions and powers of the church.
The purpose of his work—of whose novelty he was clearly
conscious—was to Marsilius that of denouncing this
urgent danger which menaced all nations and states, and
of examining the proper basis and functions of authority.
Hence his task fell into two main parts: it was first necessary to examine the essence and nature of human fellowship, and the rules which relate to it, in a word, the problem of the state; and then to proceed to examine the
essence and nature of the church, its government and
power. These two separate arguments roughly correspond
to the two main sections of the *Defensor Pacis, Dictio I* and
Dictio II; the third section (*Dictio III*) is simply a summary of the conclusions reached in the first two. No doubt

---

[1] *Defensor Pacis*, I, i, § 3: 'singularis et occulta valde, qua Romanum
imperium dudum laboravit, laboratque continuo, vehementer contagiosa, nil
minus et prona serpere in reliquas omnes civilitates et regna ipsorumque iam
plurima sui aviditate temptavit invadere.'

the whole argumentation centres upon the second part of the work, and it is in it that the boldness of Marsilius's thought is fully disclosed to us, as it was to contemporaries. We have here, in fact, not only the most radical Marsilian doctrine of the essence of religious organization, but the vindication of the power of the state with regard to it. Yet the necessary premiss of that reconstruction is already contained in the first part of the work, in the theory of the state which is there set forward on a mainly Aristotelian and heathen basis. This is the real foundation of Marsilius's thought, and it is for this reason that, as Professor Scholz has emphasized, 'everything depends on a proper understanding of the first part, that is on the understanding of the use which Marsilius makes of the Aristotelian doctrine'.

Essentially Aristotelian is the theory of the origin and attributes of political organization which is expounded in the first chapters of *Dictio I*. The state is a natural organism, rooted, like the simpler forms of domestic community or the larger types of economic relationship, in social experience, though as a *perfecta communitas* it is in its essence and ends entirely different from all other forms of human association. This assertion of the natural and not conventional origin of the state, appears to render baseless the opinion of many interpreters—and even Gierke is among them—who have thought it possible to reckon Marsilius among the theorists of a social contract. Some traces, it is true, can be found even in Marsilius, such as we have also seen in Aquinas, of the older doctrine of a contrast between an original *status innocentiae* and the actual conditions of mankind, which have made civil government necessary as *humani casus remedium*; but on the whole there can be no doubt that it is the Aristotelian treatment of the origin and foundation of the state which dominates his thought. The state was to Marsilius, as it had been to Aristotle, the *communitas perfecta* endowed with a *sufficientia per se*: it originates *vivendi gratia*, but it exists *gratia bene vivendi*. But also Marsilius, as already St. Thomas Aquinas and several other medieval Aristotelians, felt it necessary to enlarge the Aristotelian notion of πόλις so as to be able to apply it to the different types of states of his age. These are the *civitas* and the *regnum*. The latter comprises

'a number of cities or provinces under one rule. Looked on in this light, the kingdom does not differ from the city as a type of political body, but only as regards size.'[1]

In a further chapter (XVII) he mentions the problem of the Empire, but does not give a definite statement of his own opinion, and limits himself to remarking that the comparative convenience of a unity or of a plurality of governments in the world can be a matter of discussion. It has been pointed out that this evasion of the problem amounts very likely to an unfavourable attitude towards the idea of a universal empire. Some interpreters have gone so far as to see in it a tacit allusion to Dante, as if Marsilius might have preferred not to discuss his authority openly. It is enough, however, to notice that Marsilius's own notion of the state is somehow elastic enough to comprise and justify even the larger types of political organization, which were still formed of semi-autonomous units, such as the German empire or the kingdom of France.

Marsilius again follows Aristotle in regarding the state

[1] *Defensor Pacis*, I, ii, § 2: 'pluralitatem civitatum seu provinciarum sub uno regimine contentarum; secundum quam acceptionem non differt regnum a civitate in politiae specie, sed magis secundum quantitatem.'

as an organism composed of elements or *partes*, each one with a function of its own in the life of the state. These elements or *partes* are, according to Aristotle, six: *agricultura*, *artificium*, *militaris*, *pecuniativa*, *sacerdotium*, *et iudicialis seu consiliativa*. (The last one is also usually called the *pars principans* or *principatus*.) Such a distinction of offices or functions has primarily a natural foundation, which is nothing else than the natural inequality of men (*causa materialis*), but it has also and especially a human or, in other words, a political origin, inasmuch as it appears to be practically established by the will of man (*causa formalis* or *efficiens*), and is in fact the creation of a supreme human will, which Marsilius calls the *humanus legislator*. It is this will which creates, distinguishes, and separates[1] these various classes or orders, by first forming or establishing the ruling class or *pars principans*; and then, through it as an instrument, moulding all the others, including the *sacerdotium* or priestly order. It can be said that around these three terms and their mutual relationship—the *principatus*, the *sacerdotium*, and, behind and above these, the *legislator humanus*—centres the whole argument and the whole discussion of the *Defensor Pacis*.

It is thus possible to distinguish in Marsilius's political system two different problems: the problem of the form of government, and the abstract scheme which constitutes the necessary structure of the state. In his summary and analysis of the different forms of *principatus*, that is of government, Marsilius followed Aristotle very closely and repeated the traditional Aristotelian classification. His preference seems to be for some sort of limited monarchy (*regalis monarchia*), whose distinguishing features are elective origin and dependence on the law. Thus far,

---

[1] I am quoting from Professor McIlwain's excellent summary.

there is nothing exceptionally new in Marsilius's position, which plainly corresponds to the normal constitutional ideas of the Middle Ages. The novelty and radicalism of Marsilius seems rather to consist in his assertion that not only the establishment of a particular type of government, but also the designation of the person or persons which are called to exercise it, and, more important still, the framing of law as the 'forma, secundum quam civiles actus omnes regulari debent'—in short, the whole structure of the body politic—depends on one supreme and creative will, the will of the *legislator humanus*. And inasmuch as this will is, according to Marsilius, the will of the community, Marsilius's doctrine has been interpreted as containing an anticipation of the doctrine of popular sovereignty. In Gierke's words, whatever be the form of government, the structure of Marsilius's state remains unvaried, and it is the scheme of democratic radicalism. In this bold vindication of democracy lies, according to a widely diffused interpretation, one of the signs of the extraordinary novelty and modernism of Marsilius's thought.

An interpretation such as this must be subject, in my opinion, to much and substantial qualification. The meaning of Marsilius's doctrine is not so plain and obvious as appears at first sight. This is evident from the long and careful discussions which have been made by Marsilian students of the characteristic phrase, which recurs in the *Defensor Pacis* every time mention is made of the human legislator: the *legislator humanus* is constantly described as the *populus seu civium universitas, aut eius valentior pars*. I do not propose to give even a summary of the several interpretations which have been given of the expression *valentior pars*; it is enough to notice here that the recent critical reconstruction of the Marsilian text has

enabled the student entirely to exclude the older interpretation, which had been accepted by Gierke, that the
phrase *valentior pars* implied a recognition merely of
numerical majority. The text, as it has now been established, is clear and explicit: the *valentior pars* must be
determined 'considerata quantitate personarum et quali-
tate in communitate'. It was simply the omission of all
reference to quality in the *editio princeps* of 1522 which led
to the misinterpretation. Thus it is clear that in his determination of the *valentior pars*, which was to represent if
need be the whole community, Marsilius introduced
besides the notion of number that of quality. The question
of conciliating the two apparently contradictory principles
of number and quality, and of retracing the possible
sources of Marsilius's teaching on that point, is essentially an historical problem. It can only be solved by
means of an accurate study of the complex development
of the theory of representation in the political and ecclesiastical organizations of the Middle Ages. But from a
merely theoretical point of view it can be remarked that
the introduction of the notion of quality amounts to a
very important qualification of the presumed democratic
character of Marsilius's doctrine, and of the so-called principle of popular sovereignty too often mentioned in this
regard. A system which is based not upon equality, but
upon inequality, in which votes must not only be counted,
but weighed, cannot properly be termed democratic. In
the same *Defensor*, moreover, we can find an open condemnation of democracy as a corrupt form of government;
for a democratic community does not exercise its power
'secundum proportionem convenientem'. In other words,
democracy contradicts that principle of proportional
equality which is, according to Aristotle the proper foun-

dation of a good government. The common character of
such government is no doubt that power should be exer-
cised for the common good (*commune conferens*), and that
it should be based upon the will, that is upon the consent,
of the subjects (*iuxta subditorum voluntatem sive consensum*).
But we would search in vain the whole *Defensor* for a vindication of that principle which forms the real foundation
of the modern doctrine of popular sovereignty: the principle of the original and natural equality of all the members
of the community, and thus of the value of the individual
as the ultimate source of power and the bearer of an equal
fraction of the sovereign authority.

If the widely held view of the implications of the
Marsilian theory requires some modification, so also does
the view that Marsilius was the first to lay down this
theory. It is, in fact, characteristic that even those who
more openly assert this novelty have felt it necessary to
point out the possible sources of Marsilius's teaching. I
have already had occasion, in my preceding lecture, to
mention these different sources of the medieval doctrine
of the ultimate derivation of power from the community.
The usual interpretation refers Marsilius's theory to the
Roman doctrine of the transmission of power from the
people to the prince. But this interpretation is shaken by
the fact that Marsilius appears to have been very little
acquainted with, or influenced by, Roman law. Marsilius,
indeed, was in no way setting out a new and revolutionary
democratic doctrine, but was rather expressing, though
in more drastic and unqualified terms, the normal judgement and practice of the Middle Ages. To emphasize
further the traditional character of Marsilius's teaching,
one may add that his insistence upon consent as the
justification of authority, and hence upon the necessary

derivation of political power from a merely human source, the community, does not exclude the ultimate divine or rather sacred character of power itself. He accepted this doctrine from the teaching of St. Paul (Rom. xiii. 1); and there is more than one reference to the traditional Christian teaching in the further developments of the *Defensor*, whenever the religious duty of obedience is mentioned.

Another modern doctrine which some interpreters have seen in this section of Marsilius's teaching is that of the 'separation of powers'. Marsilius distinguishes and opposes the *legislator humanus*, that is the 'civium universitas seu eius pars valentior', to the *pars principans*. The latter is conceived only as a part or secondary function, 'quasi instrumentalis et executiva', having as its task merely the *executio legalium*, or the application of the law. Law can be established only by the *legislator*; it is the duty of the *pars principans* to govern in accordance with it. But if we look more carefully at the teaching of Marsilius, it is clear that the functions of the *legislator* on the one hand and of the *pars principans* on the other correspond only remotely to the modern conceptions of legislative and executive power. The function of the *pars principans* is not merely executive, for it includes a judicial power and several other functions which are far from being clearly defined; Marsilius also calls the *pars principans, iudicialis* and *consiliativa*. This *pars principans* corresponds rather to the medieval conception of the ruler as the tutor and warrant of a law, to which he also is subject, like all the other members of the community, than to the modern executive. Nor has the Marsilian *legislator* (who, as Professor McIlwain has shown, literally corresponds to the Aristotelian νομο θέτης) a merely legislative function. The *legislator* is *principatus institutor*, as well as *legislator*; among his powers there is, moreover, that of controlling, and if necessary of punishing the prince if he abuses his function. In short, if we are to use after all a modern vocabulary, we might say with Professor McIlwain that the power which belongs, according to Marsilius, to the *legislator humanus* is a 'constituent' rather than a 'legislative' power; or perhaps it is better still to acknowledge frankly that, in Marsilius's system, there is no place for any abstract or mechanical distinction of 'powers' within the state, since all power ultimately goes back to the *legislator humanus*, who thus appears as the real and supreme creative force within the state and of the state itself.

But with this last recognition we are, in fact, brought back to our starting-point, to the fundamental principle laid down by Marsilius, that the whole structure of the body politic depends on the will of the *legislator humanus*. Now it seems to me that it is precisely here that we must turn to retrace the real 'novelty' of Marsilius's thought. His starting-point is no doubt traditional: it is the principle that the source of authority lies in the community. But the interpretation of this principle, the consequences which he contrived to draw from it with extraordinary logic and coherence, bear an undeniable mark of boldness and of novelty. To appreciate at its true value the originality of Marsilius's position we must examine the section of his theory of the state which best illustrates the break with the traditional ideas, viz. his theory of law. This particular section of Marsilius's teaching has not yet received at the hands of students (except perhaps in M. de Lagarde's brilliant, but not very sympathetic summary) the attention which it undoubtedly deserves.

The problem of law, of its foundation and character, is the object of careful and lengthy discussion in both the first and second parts of the *Defensor Pacis*.[1] The notion of right (*ius*) presupposes, according to Marsilius, the existence of law, the existence, that is, of an objective rule of human conduct. Such rules fall into two great categories, divine law and human law, and all *ius* flows from them exclusively: the notion of a *ius naturale* in addition to them can thus only be 'equivocal', since it cannot be grounded upon any ascertained rule. We shall soon realize the full consequences of this surprising attitude of Marsilius with regard to a notion which, as we have seen, had recently become with St. Thomas the key-stone of the whole system of medieval ethics.

Let us examine further the notion of law. Of all human actions, Marsilius remarks, 'adinventae sunt quaedam regulae seu mensurae vel habitus.' Among these many possible rules, generally called by the name of law, human and divine laws can be distinguished by some common character: the sanction, reward, or punishment which accompanies them, the power or *potentia coactiva* which imposes their observance. Thus both undoubtedly appear as coercive precepts, but with an important difference: the coercive character of the human law bears its full efficiency already in this world, while that of divine law is reserved for a future life. Hence it follows that, from a purely human or worldly or 'political' point of view ('in statu et pro statu vitae praesentis') the divine law (*evangelica lex*) can only appear as an ethical teaching ('rationem habet magis doctrinae speculativae aut operativae'), not as a properly efficient law, for the obvious reason that 'per evangelicam doctrinam seu legem nemo cogi praecipitur in hoc saeculo'. The typical Marsilian attitude towards Revelation, which has been described, is here clearly apparent.

---

[1] *Dictio I*, ch. x, xi, xii; *Dictio II*, ch. viii, ix, xii.

This, very briefly, is the sum of Marsilius's theory of law: I have omitted on purpose the complex apparatus of distinctions which accompany it. Let me call your attention to the particular conception of law which it implies. Leaving aside all the secondary meanings of the word law, the essence of law appears to lie in its 'imperative' and 'coercive' character. Law presupposes the *actus imperandi*, and it is from this that it draws its value.

It might almost be Hobbes's or Austin's conception of law; it is certainly the exact reverse of the Thomist conception. While St. Thomas, as we know, had seen the very essence of law in its rational character, that is in its substance or 'content', Marsilius emphasizes the 'formal' element, that is the will of the legislator, who lays down the law and gives it its actual value. This principle is fully developed in the tenth chapter of *Dictio I*. Here, after an account of the several meanings of the word *lex*, Marsilius remarks that a law can be considered as simply a definition of right and wrong, or else as a command to act in a definite manner: 'et hoc modo considerata propriissime lex vocatur et est.' Therefore the several rules which relate to the conduct of men are not properly laws, 'nisi de ipsarum observatione datum fuerit praeceptum coactivum, seu latae fuerint per modum praecepti'. No doubt, if a law is to be a good law (*perfecta*), it is necessary that it should embody a principle of justice and of common good ('iustum et civile conferens'). It may sometimes happen, as is the case among non-civilized nations, 'in regionibus barbarorum',[1] that laws command things contrary to justice; in this case, though having the *forma debita* of coercive precepts, they lack the *debita conditio* which makes a

---

[1] The meaning of this expression has given rise to different conjectures among recent interpreters.

perfect law. This seems an important qualification, and clearly shows that the 'formal' element, the *praeceptum coactivum*, is not the only constituent element of law, and that its content or substance must also be taken into account, and valued with reference to an ideal of justice. Yet, if we consider more closely Marsilius's doctrine, this apparent reservation, which seems at first sight to contain an acknowledgement of the priority of justice with regard to the law of the state, turns out to have a very different meaning, and amounts to a further break with the traditional and Thomist point of view. For, according to Marsilius, the definition and valuation of that very element of justice which must be embodied in law, entirely depends on the will of the legislator, which is itself also the source of the law's imperative character. Marsilius's theory of law thus appears to be directly connected with the fundamental premisses which have been examined above. It is here, in fact, that we find what is, according to him, the main argument in favour of power belonging to the community. Only the whole community can adequately value what is just and consonant to the common good, and express it in the form of law; reciprocally, only what the community has laid down in the form of law can and must be the supreme measure of justice. Human decision is raised to nothing less than a standard of truth, and the reason of this is stated in a sentence which has an almost utilitarian flavour: 'quoniam illius veritas certius iudicatur, et ipsius communis utilitas diligentius attenditur, ad quod tota intendit civium universitas intellectu et affectu.'[1] This expression is no doubt reminiscent of formulas which are current in medieval political literature, such as the well-known principle 'quod omnes tangit ab omnibus appro-

[1] *Dictio I*, ch. xii, § 5 and § 8.

betur'; but in the context which I have described it assumes an entirely new meaning. Clearly, we have here a notion of the sovereignty of the 'general will' which reminds us even more of Rousseau than of Bodin or of Austin.

However this may be, we are certainly in an entirely different world from that of St. Thomas. There is nothing left of the Thomist idea that the 'state', however 'sovereign', is subject to an eternal and absolute order of values, expressed in the body of divine and natural law. The state is the source of law, and its law has to be obeyed not only because it is the only rule to be endowed with coercive power, but because it is in itself the expression of justice. There is no place here for the Christian idea of divided allegiance, nor for the defence of fundamental values against the all-powerful will of the state. No doubt divine law still remains in existence; and, as Lagarde humorously remarks, there is one text especially which causes Marsilius some trouble, when it is said (Acts iv. 19) that it is better to obey God than man. Marsilius is indeed willing to admit that the Christian is not bound to obey 'contra legem salutis aeternae'. But that does not shake in the least the main bulk of his argument. On the contrary, resuming long-forgotten arguments, which the Reformation was to develop, Marsilius claims the moral support of the revealed law in favour of obedience, if not actually of unquestioning obedience. In fact, as he points out, any trespass against human law is a trespass against divine law, which prescribes the duty of secular obedience; while, on the other hand, human law may regard with indifference that which is an act of disobedience to the divine law alone.[1] This is the point: since human law has also the

---

[1] *Defensor Pacis*, II, ix, § 11: see below, p. 76.

might of this world on its side, and is therefore the only law worthy of the name, it will always have its way in the end, it will impose itself upon the subject, *etiam non volentem*. In other words, even though the rules of religion (those of natural law are, as we know, out of the question) may contain or imply a different notion of justice, a different scale of values from that of the state, these notions and values have no properly legal character, except in so far as the state embodies them in its own law, and gives them coercive force. Otherwise, as Marsilius caustically remarks, they are mere anticipations of a reward or punishment in another life, but certainly not in this. We shall see the full consequences of this attitude in a later connexion.

But what are we to think of this attitude in itself, and by what name are we to describe it? The traditional doctrine of the power of the community has clearly undergone a radical change at the hands of Marsilius. And yet, for the reasons which we have seen, it seems inadequate to speak of a theory of popular sovereignty. We have been led into a sea of pure metaphysics. The very notion of sovereignty, at least in its current legal meaning, seems inadequate, though it is undoubtedly there. Law, which the Thomist had conceived as prior to the state, as both a condition and limit of political power, now appears as the very creation of the state, as the outflow and test of its sovereignty. We are confronted, according to M. de Lagarde, with a 'positivist' conception of law; but this conception can equally well, or perhaps better, be termed 'voluntarist', for it is this emphasis upon the paramountcy of will which really breaks up the Thomist conception. One would also be tempted to speak of a 'humanization' of politics, and it is perhaps this ugly word which best succeeds in marking the dominant character of Marsilius's thought. Yet we are still far away from the Renaissance, and Marsilius's pedantic veneration and interpretation of Aristotle is more reminiscent of the schoolman than of the humanist. The 'secret' of Marsilius still eludes us, but it is not until we have examined the full bulk of his argument, and tested his revolutionary reconstruction of the Christian ideal, that we can properly realize its astonishing complexity.

IV

MARSILIUS OF PADUA

(continued)

MARSILIUS'S theory of the Church is usually considered the most original and revolutionary part of his work, and it has from the outset, as appears from the unparalleled violence of Papal denunciations, been the centre of passionate discussion. It is on this section of Marsilius's teaching that the modern student also usually centres his attention, as if detecting in the radical reversal of the traditional medieval positions the more important and personal contribution of Marsilius to the development of political thought.

'Dès que nous abordons l'aspect négatif de l'œuvre marsilienne— writes M. de Lagarde in his usual brilliant style—nous voyons s'affirmer une rigueur logique, une force d'argumentation et un radicalisme auxquels ses premiers essais ne nous avaient pas habitués. Que ce soit dans la critique de l'institution ecclésiastique, dans la théorie des usurpations reprochées à l'Église, dans celle, enfin, de son incompatibilité avec toute notion d'ordre social ou politique, à toutes les étapes de sa pensée, nous allons retrouver l'annonce géniale des idées qui ont été et restent encore la base permanente de la lutte menée par la cité laïque contre l'Église.'

The theory of the Church and of its relation to political authority occupies, in fact, the whole second part of the *Defensor Pacis*, which covers more than three times the number of pages of the first. The modern literature on the argument can be said to be more or less in the same proportion, and I have therefore no ambition to attempt a complete reconstruction of Marsilius's theory, or of the actual state of the learned discussions relating to it. Once again I shall limit myself to some short remarks on what I consider to be the main issues of Marsilius's position.

First of all, as I remarked in the previous lecture, however new and different are the ground and arguments which are taken up in the second part of the *Defensor Pacis*, their premisses are already contained in the first part, in that theory of the state which has been briefly analysed. If this be granted, we have here no doubt an important argument, drawn from internal evidence, for settling the much discussed question of the authorship of the *Defensor Pacis*. This is not, however, the point I am concerned with, since the most authoritative interpreters have now almost unanimously agreed to attribute the authorship of the whole work to Marsilius alone, whatever may have been his association with the Frenchman John of Jandun, who shared with him the condemnation for heresy. The point is of even greater importance from a theoretical angle, inasmuch as upon it depends any exact discussion of the question which, as I have tried to show, is the crucial issue of Marsilius's thought. What is the real significance of the Marsilian revival of the Aristotelian conception of the state, and what influence had it on the solution of the essentially Christian problem, unknown to the Ancients, of the relation between religious and political organization?

It is in the first part of the *Defensor Pacis* that we find the first approach to the problem of religious organization. Priesthood is there described as a 'part' or necessary function of the state. Marsilius's argument is typical of his attitude towards religious questions: he might almost be an unbeliever of the present day. He points out that mankind soon realized the necessity for some sort of priestly function and organization, a *pars sacerdotalis*, for the well-being of the state. Even those among the ancient philosophers who did not believe in eternal life recognized the convenience of enforcing human laws with religious sanctions, with the promise of eternal salvation or the menace of eternal punishment. They saw the enormous advantage which could be drawn from this idea, for the human legislator cannot control and regulate every human action, while nothing can be said to escape the eye of God. The idea of God had to be invented in some way for the well-being and good of the state—the words are not mine, they are to be found in the fifth chapter of the *Dictio Prima*. Thus also the heathen had a clergy. Marsilius is willing, however, to admit that, with the advent of Christianity as the true religion, conditions are evidently changed, and a different explanation can be given of the necessity of divine laws and of priesthood. It is interesting to notice that he recurs to the idea of sin to prove the necessity of divine law as a remedy for human corruption. In the Christian state, therefore (*communitas fidelium*), the purpose and justification of the clergy must be sought in the law of the Gospel and in the establishment of a 'discipline' in accordance with it.[1]

It appears from these premises, laid down from the very beginning, that for Marsilius the religious functions of the priesthood have also a political basis. There is, in other words, a 'natural' foundation of priesthood as necessary to the state, independent of the truth of religion in itself. And even after the advent of the true religion, of Christianity, though the functions of the priesthood may have changed with regard to eternal life, with regard to the state and from the purely political standpoint, the value of priesthood has remained the same: it is a part

[1] *Defensor Pacis,* I, chaps. v and vi.

of the political structure and is subject to its laws. As such, the clergy, the *pars sacerdotalis* in the body politic, is entirely dependent on the government of that same body, that is on the *pars principans*. It must, therefore, be regulated and controlled by the prince, and cannot possess, in any of its stages, any sort of coercive power.[1]

It is thus possible to reconstruct, with the help of the *Dictio I* alone, the main lines of Marsilius's theory with regard to the position of the 'church' within the 'state' (I wish to draw your attention to the inverted commas). According to this theory the clergy are nothing but a 'part' of the state, which must be ruled by the prince on the same lines as all other parts or classes which compose the body politic. Their only function is that of teaching and preaching the Word of God, and of administering the Sacraments; these are purely spiritual functions in which the secular ruler has not to interfere. But in all things pertaining to the *officium principatus coactivi* the clergy as well as all the other parts of the community must be subject to the authority and government of the State.

In the *Dictio II* Marsilius simply shifts the discussion from the standpoint of the state to that of the church. It is clear that the problem of the church was to him altogether a different problem from that of the priesthood or clergy. The latter he considered to have a necessary function, both from a political and a religious point of view; but the former raised the whole problem of the actual organization of the Christian ideal. Hence, while in the first part the highest authority could be granted to the Philosopher, in the second the discussion necessarily involved a close and careful interpretation of Holy Writ.

The Marsilian definition of the church has been the

---

[1] *Defensor Pacis*, I, chaps. xv and xix.

object of careful analysis, and its importance and meaning can obviously only be valued in relation to the whole development of ecclesiology during the Middle Ages and the period of the Reformation. 'The word church is used . . . for the whole body of faithful who believe in and invoke the name of Christ, and for all the parts of this body in every community, even in the household.'[1] Similarly the term *viri ecclesiastici* ought to be applied to all the faithful of Christ, as well priests as non-priests;[2] there is, in fact, no difference whatever, either personal or substantial, between clergy and laity. It may well be, as has been said many times, an anticipation of the Protestant doctrine of the priesthood of all believers; it is certainly a severe blow to the sacramental character of the medieval and Catholic Church. Let us not forget, however, even in this connexion, Professor Scholz's warning against the error of attributing to religious motives what may well only be an expression of 'a purely secular and political standpoint'. Marsilius's definition, which might, in another context, be taken as an expression of religious feeling, remains much more in the line of legal argumentation than in that of any religious revivalism. It is a new and decisive argument in his struggle against clericalism; and it is, in fact, with the help of this new definition, together with the principle already laid down of the merely spiritual functions of priesthood, that he immediately sets himself to demolish one by one the bitterly contested positions

---

[1] *Defensor Pacis*, II, ch. ii, § 3: 'dicitur hoc nomen *ecclesia* . . . de universitate fidelium credentium et invocantium nomen Christi, et de huius universitatis partibus omnibus in quacumque communitate, etiam domestica.' It is important to compare this definition with the parallel one in the *Defensor Minor*, ch. xv. 8.

[2] *Defensor Pacis*, loc. cit.: 'viri ecclesiastici secundum hanc verissimam et propriissimam significationem sunt et dici debent omnes Christi fideles, tam sacerdotes, quam non-sacerdotes. . . .'

of the Roman hierarchy. The discussion is tedious enough, and I may be forgiven for turning straight to the main argument under discussion: the problem of the actual organization of the church, after the whole structure based on the pretended powers of the 'Bishop of Rome' has been torn to pieces. What is the new order which must take the place of the old one, and how is the church as *universitas fidelium* to ensure its life and organization?

The principle which ought to preside over the organization of the church, and to inspire and determine its life, is, according to Marsilius, exactly the same as the principle which determines the structure of political organization. It is the principle that the source of all power is the community. After the close of the Apostolic age, in which Christ Himself had personally conferred his power on the Apostles, when the first Christian communities began to be established, there can be no doubt, in Marsilius's view, that the choice and nomination of the 'ministers' of religion passed entirely into the hands of the community:[1]

'I wish to show that . . . the communities of the faithful being now perfected, the appointment and choice of a prelate (whether of a greater one who is called a bishop, of a lesser one whom they call a priest, or of other lesser ones) belongs and ought to belong to the whole body of believers of that place (*universa eius loci fidelium multitudo*), or to him or those to whom the said body has granted the power of making these appointments.'

Universa eius loci fidelium multitudo: i.e. the several Christian communities; and inasmuch as in the Christian

---

[1] *Ibid.*, II xvii, § 8: 'Ostendere volo quod . . . communitatibus fidelium iam perfectis, huius institutionis seu determinationis praesidis (sive maioris, quem vocant *episcopum*, sive minorum, quos *curatos sacerdotes* appellant), similiter et reliquorum minorum, causa factiva immediata sit seu esse debeat universa eius loci fidelium multitudo per suam electionem seu voluntatem expressam, aut ille vel illi, cui vel quibus iamdicta multitudo harum institutionum auctoritatem concesserit.'

state the *communitas fidelium* exactly coincides with the *communitas civium*, the ultimate source of power, both in temporal and in spiritual matters, is the same. Thus the government of the church, like that of the state, must go back to the *legislator humanus*. It is thus in the *legislator humanus*, henceforward considered by Marsilius as *fidelis*, that all power, spiritual and temporal, is concentrated. The condition necessary for this to happen is, of course, that the state and its government should both be Christian; where the state is not of this quality, the *communitas civium* and the *communitas fidelium* no longer coincide, and the church will thus appear as a different body from the state, and be governed and administered independently. But it is important to notice that religious unity and orthodoxy are to Marsilius's eye the normal conditions of the Christian world, and the expression *communitas perfecta fidelium* which he uses to designate the Christian state bears evidence of this coincidence, in a single body, of both 'state' and 'church'.[1]

Marsilius's theory thus leads to a complete dependency of the church on the sovereign *legislator humanus*. Further, it has the serious consequence of imperilling the universal character of the church itself, which appears to be split up as it were into the multiplicity of the single *communitates perfectae fidelium*. I do not propose to examine the complex theory which is developed by Marsilius to meet this difficulty and which is undoubtedly marked by a certain uneasiness and ambiguity. It is enough to remark that Marsilius nowhere refers to the idea of the 'invisible' church, which was to be resorted to and emphasized by the Protestant Reformers as a means of preserving its unity at least on a religious and spiritual plane. His approach to the problem is again essentially legal and,

[1] *Defensor Pacis*, II, ch. xvii.

I should say, constitutional. The value of the Conciliar theory which he constructs on a democratic and Erastian basis and its relation with later developments are problems which I am not competent to discuss in this place. I have, however, said enough to attempt a valuation of Marsilius's position, if not with regard to later theory and practice, at least in its relation to the traditional medieval interpretation of the Christian ideal and the issues which this raised.

The novelty of Marsilius's position appears first of all in the fact that, as I have already pointed out, while the defenders of secular government had so far been contented with a merely defensive position, the *Defensor Pacis* resolutely moves to attack. The traditional 'Gelasian' principle of the distinction and co-operation of the two powers necessary to the right government of the Christian world, which had provided the ground for such opposition to Papal claims, as that of Dante or John of Paris, is here openly challenged. Marsilius's whole effort can be said to be directed against this traditional duality which, as we have seen, the medieval mind had striven to reduce to unity on a higher and mystical plane. And yet this *reductio ad absurdum* of the medieval dilemma was not without a precedent. The attack on the traditional duality was common both to Marsilius and to the doctrine, which he so violently opposed, that all power, both spiritual and temporal, was brought to unity in the *plenitudo potestatis* of the Pope. The issue was in both cases the same, and it is the issue of sovereignty. It is, if we are to avoid using a term which is not yet there, the logic of unity. This new logic, which is the real strength of Marsilius's argument, had been already applied to the demonstration of the universal monarchy of the church. It is clearly laid down in the bull *Unam Sanctam* and in the writings in support of

Boniface's claims. Nor even was this, as has been believed for a long time, a new and revolutionary doctrine: for, as Prof. Powicke points out, it had hardened in half a century of desperate struggle, which had finally led to the conclusion that, 'of two irreconcilable powers, one must be the greater, the sovereign'.[1] It was the work of legally trained and subtle Italian minds, though it had aroused the indignation and the deep religious feelings of another great Italian, Dante Alighieri. But the effects of this new logic of unity were in truth devastating for Dante's and for the whole medieval ideal. It involved, in Prof. Previté-Orton's words, the cloudy emergence of novel, or at least unaccustomed, conceptions for which a strict terminology had not yet been invented or revived. It contained, in fact, a notion which was to work havoc with the medieval duality: the abstract notion of absolute sovereignty. It is this notion which Marsilius struggled to express, and which gives to his work its extraordinary coherence and originality, even though he undoubtedly shared the merit of the 'discovery' with other and very different writers of his age.

But when we turn to examine the proper field in which the new and revolutionary doctrine found its application, we cannot but be struck by the fact that this very field was, as was already the case with the so-called 'theocratic' doctrine, still much more medieval than modern. For, indeed, if the abstract logic of sovereignty enabled Marsilius to assert the absurdity of a dualism which Boniface had already before him declared to be 'monstrous', the premiss of his whole system was still that of the necessary unity of religious and political life within a truly Christian society. This unity, indeed, was to Marsilius so complete, that, as we have seen, 'state' and 'church' cannot in any way be

1 *The Christian life in the Middle Ages and other essays*, Oxford, 1935, p. 56.

conceived as separate bodies. They coincide completely
in the one *respublica christiana*, or, to use Marsilius's words,
in the *communitas perfecta fidelium*. Thus, whatever be the
value of the idea of the *respublica christiana* for the interpretation of medieval political ideas, we certainly have
some ground to see in its acceptance by Marsilius a mark
of its traditional character. For it is this acceptance which
explains why, with all his 'modernism', Marsilius was unable to rise to a notion which still remained unknown to
the medieval mind: the notion of a deep and far-reaching
difference between religious and political obligation. For
him, as for the traditional medieval doctrine, the 'state'
cannot exist without the 'church', nor the 'church' without
the 'state'. He refers, it is true, to their possible distinction
and independence in his analysis of the conditions of religious organization in a non-Christian or heathen society,
but the reference is incidental, and only confirms the
necessary coincidence of the religious and political community in a thoroughly Christian society. It is precisely
the application to this social structure of the principle of the
absolute sovereignty of the 'state' which led him to deny
all possible independence to the church, as the supporters
of theocracy had denied all independence to the state in
the name of the sovereignty of the church. Theocracy
meant the absorption of state into church; Marsilianism
the absorption of church into state; but this in turn
necessarily implied a degradation of religion to a mere
instrumentum regni. The logical consequences of this
position are all clearly apparent in Marsilius's teaching.

To understand these consequences in their proper meaning it is necessary to recall briefly Marsilius's theory of
the relation between human and divine law. According to
Marsilius, as you will probably remember, divine law is

essentially and solely concerned with religious values, that is, with eternal salvation. It is therefore entirely devoid of any coercive character: not only because the *coactiva potestas* is an exclusive concern of the human legislator, but also—and this is very important—because compulsion by force would be inconsistent with its religious and spiritual end: 'nam coactis nihil spirituale proficit ad salutem aeternam.'[1] But human and divine laws do not only differ, according to Marsilius, in their different sanctions, they also and mainly differ with regard to their comparative spheres of action. The moral and religious sphere which is regulated by the divine law is, in Marsilius's opinion, a larger sphere than that of the human law; inasmuch as divine law really considers human conduct in all its aspects, while human law can only consider it in its objective, i.e. external aspect. Hence it follows that, as we have already seen, any trespass against human law implies a trespass against the moral or divine order, while, on the other hand, not every trespass against the moral or divine order is a violation of the positive or human one. The reason for this, as Marsilius openly acknowledges, is that a control of internal motives is impossible to the human legislator.[2] 'Conscience', here again, appears to be free from worldly sanctions. All this seems very liberal and modern, and Marsilius has, in fact, been hailed as a prophet also in this respect. Does he not here anticipate the modern idea of freedom of conscience, and the modern distinction

---

[1] *Defensor Pacis*, II, ix, § 4.

[2] *Ibid.*, § 11: 'Transgressor humanae legis quasi ut in pluribus peccat in Legem Divinam, licet e converso non sic. Quoniam multi sunt actus in quibus committens aut omittens peccat contra Legem Divinam, quae de hiis praecipit de quibus humana lex frustra praeciperet: quales sunt quos pridem diximus ... qui alicui adesse vel non inesse probari nequeunt, cum tamen Deum latere non possint.'

between morals and politics? Let us reserve our judgement until we have inquired more carefully.

One would expect Marsilius, having thus emphatically reasserted the purely spiritual character of the divine law and the purely spiritual mission of priesthood, to acknowledge a clear-cut distinction between the sphere of morals and religion and that of politics. But that is not, and cannot be, the case in Marsilius's system, as we can readily infer if we remember the premisses of that system. The intimate connexion it presupposes between the religious and the political orders, or shall we say, the very acceptance of the traditional idea of the *respublica christiana*, make such a clear-cut distinction impossible and even unthinkable. In Marsilius's Christian commonwealth, in his *communitas perfecta fidelium*, it is impossible that a trespass against the laws of religion should not produce temporal, besides spiritual consequences.

This necessary interaction between the religious and the political sphere is clearly apparent in Marsilius's treatment of heresy and its punishment. Marsilius is here entirely in the traditional line. Excommunication must needs have temporal consequences. If religion and politics, church and state, were distinct and independent, a purely spiritual punishment, such as the exclusion of the heretic from the community of the faithful, would be of no interest politically. But to Marsilius such exclusion necessarily brings, *ipso facto*, an exclusion *etiam civili communione atque commoditate* (II. vi. 12). Such a consequence is inevitable in a system in which the religious and the political community completely coincide. But this is not all. For Marsilius acknowledges the necessity, in the orthodox state, of heresy being punished, though of course he denies any *coactiva potestas* to the clergy in this respect.

'We do not, however, mean to say that it is incongruous for heretics or unbelievers in general to be coerced but that the authority to do this, if it be permitted, belongs solely to the *legislator humanus*.'[1] The phrase 'if it be permitted' (*si liceat hoc fieri*) is curious and significant. One would almost be tempted to see in it a hint of Marsilius's scepticism, a glcam of a possible system of toleration. Not less significant is the fact that the phrase is entirely dropped in the *editio princeps* of 1522, when the *Defensor* was published as a challenge to the Roman Church.[2] Protestantism, at least at this stage, had even less sympathy than medieval Catholicism with the idea of toleration. It is clear, however, that Marsilius did not exclude persecution, but on the contrary considered it as normal. His innovation—if it be an innovation at all—lies in his main contention that persecution, as implying actual punishment in this world, cannot be grounded merely on divine law, but must be enforced by the law of the State:

'It is not because of a trespass simply against divine law, that a man is punished by the prince. There are many mortal sins and sins against divine law, such as fornication, which the human legislator even knowingly permits, and which no bishop or priest may forbid with coercive power. But he who sins against divine law, as the heretic does, when that sin is also prohibited by human law, is punished in this world (*in hoc saeculo*) inasmuch as he sins against human law.'[3]

---

[1] *Defensor Pacis*, II, v, § 7: 'Nec tamen ex hiis dicere volumus inconveniens esse coerceri haereticos aut aliter infideles, sed auctoritatem hanc, si liceat hoc fieri, esse solius legislatoris humani.'

[2] It appears, however, to be missing in some MSS. before this.

[3] *Ibid.* x, § 7: 'Non enim propterea quod in legem divinam tantummodo peccet quis, a principante punitur. Sunt enim multa peccata mortalia et in legem divinam, ut fornicationis, quae permittit etiam scienter legislator humanus, nec coactiva potentia prohibet nec prohibere potest aut debet episcopus vel sacerdos. Sed peccans in legem divinam, haereticus scilicet, tali

Clearly, although denying the right of persecution to the church, Marsilius openly admits it at the hands of the state. The state is somehow necessarily led to persecution, inasmuch as the state is *fidelis,* inasmuch as it is founded upon religious orthodoxy and unity. Hence, necessarily, any attack on orthodoxy must appear as an attack on that unity of the state which, as we know, is the basis of Marsilius's system. Persecution, in other words, is a public necessity; heresy, as subversive of public order, can and must be punished. All depends on whether human law, that is, the state, has decided on punishment, whether the state is willing to adopt and enforce the precept of divine law, which, as we know, can as such only have a sanction in another world. All depends, in a word, on the will of the state, which is also here, as always, the paramount and decisive factor.

That a system such as the one which I have described may have appeared to contain an anticipation of religious liberty, I confess is to me a cause of bewilderment. It seems to me, on the contrary, essentially incompatible with the theory and practice of religious, and indeed of political liberalism, such as we are still accustomed to consider as one of the highest achievements of our European civilization. In fact, Marsilius's doctrine that religious opinions and beliefs cannot be enforced does not appear to be substantially different from the traditional Christian doctrine. It is the very substance of the teaching of the Church, which we can find openly stated in Gratian's *Decretum,*[1] and expressed in its full philosophical implications by St. Thomas when he declares that matters of faith cannot be the object of coercive

peccato etiam humana lege prohibito, punitur in hoc saeculo in quantum peccans in legem humanum.'   [1] I, Dist. XLV, c. 3–5.

enforcement, *quia credere voluntatis est*.[1] Indeed, this
doctrine of the freedom and inviolability of 'conscience'
is an essential part of Christianity, nor did the church
betray this principle even in an age in which all power
and authority seemed to have been centred in its hands.

But, it may be objected, Marsilius is pleading precisely
in favour of that liberty against its violation at the hands
of the medieval church. This is not the place to discuss
the historical accurateness of such an argument. You
will allow me simply to quote once again St. Thomas's
authority as expressing also in this respect the normal
medieval doctrine. St. Thomas is emphatic in his denial
that, in the exercise of their ministry, that is, in applying
the law of God, the clergy may use other weapons except
spiritual ones, 'quae quidem sunt salubres admonitiones,
devotae orationes, contra pertinaces excommunicationis
sententia'.[2] He admits, it is true, 'corporal' compulsion in
matters of faith. But, for one thing, such compulsion
cannot be used against non-Christians, such as Jews or
heathens, to oblige them to embrace the true faith, for,
as we have seen, faith is not enforceable. It may be used,
on different grounds, against the crimes of apostasy and
heresy; but in this case it is quite clear that such *coërcitio*
cannot happen 'per spiritualem potestatem Ecclesiae', but
can only be done 'per temporalem potestatem', and must
therefore be entrusted to the *brachium saeculare*. Thus,
also for St. Thomas, coercive power (*coactiva potestas*) is at
bottom incompatible with religious ministration, and is in
fact an attribute exclusively of the *potestas publica*, that is,
of the sovereign.[3]

This short review of the normal and orthodox medieval

---

[1] *Summa Theol.* 2a 2ae, q. x, a. 8.   [2] *Ibid.* 2a 2ae, q. xl, a. 2: and also q. lxiv, a. 4.
[3] *Ibid.* 2a 2ae, q. xi, a. 3; q. xxxix, a. 4; q. lx, a. 6; q. lxvii, a. 1.

doctrine, as found in St. Thomas, is enough to show that it is not possible to speak without qualification of Marsilius's modernism. His parallel assertion that faith, as an essentially spiritual value, cannot be compelled, but that heresy, as a menace to unity in Church and state and as a trespass against the moral and religious standards embodied in civil legislation, must be punished; that, in a word, religious conformity is the condition of the very existence of a Christian commonwealth; all this corresponds very closely to the medieval and Catholic doctrine of which Lord Acton has given us that brilliant analysis which you will certainly remember.[1] It is, to quote Acton's words, a theory of intolerance 'handed down from an age when unity subsisted, and when its preservation, being essential for that of society, became a necessity of state as well as a result of circumstances'.

Yet, when all this is said, it is impossible to deny that Marsilius's theory diverges, in more than one point, from the traditional doctrine. But in these points he is anything but liberal, and rather seems to lead us in an opposite direction. According to Professor Ruffini,[2] there is only a short step from Marsilius's contention that heresy must be punished not as a trespass against the law of God, but against the law of the state, to the modern doctrine that restrictions on liberty of religious opinion and organization may be imposed only in the interests of public order and security. But it is significant that Marsilius refrains from taking that step. His whole system rather implies a denial of any sort of freedom of religious organization, of any 'liberty' of the church (to use the old medieval and

[1] 'The Protestant Theory of Persecution', in *The History of Freedom and other essays*, ed. by J. N. Figgis and R. V. Laurence, London, 1909.

[2] *Religious Liberty*, English translation with a Preface by Professor J. B. Bury, London, 1912, pp. 43-5.

Catholic expression); and although no doubt such liberty implies a very different notion from that of religious freedom, it is difficult to see how the latter can be attained when the former is challenged. Marsilius's theory leads, in fact, as we have seen, to a complete absorption of the church into the state. It is here, in my opinion, that we must look for the real 'modernism' of Marsilius's position. If we are, at all costs, to see in it an anticipation of later systems and doctrines, it is certainly not the modern notion of religious liberty that we can find in it. It is much rather a notion which implies the most radical denial of any such liberty, and expresses that complete subjection of the church to the state, which was to be the outcome of the Reformation in some countries of Europe. It is the vindication of the right of several petty governments to exercise the supreme authority and control of religious matters within the boundaries of their several states, and of the duty of the subject to conform to the religion of the prince. It is, in a word, the principle of territorialism, which was to be laid down in the Peace of Augsburg more than two centuries later (1555) and finds its expression in the famous formula, *cuius regio, eius religio*. We shall have more to say on that principle in a further lecture.

But, again, it may be argued that Marsilius's theory, by vindicating the right of the state to control religious matters in the name of public order and by merely legal means, implicitly sets a limit to state action. Human or positive law, which is the only means which the state has at its disposal, can only consider, as we know, external behaviour; hence it can never extend to internal motives, nor properly infringe the freedom of conscience. But this is a very weak argument. For one thing, the border-line between 'internal' and 'external' matters, which seems so

easy to draw from a merely legal standpoint, appears in a
very different light from the point of view of religious and
moral experience. It is significant enough that the definition of these limits should have become a crucial issue of
moral philosophy from the time of the Reformation down
to our present day. But far more important still is the fact
that the argument itself can only apply to the case when
the state deliberately renounces any pretence of religious
unity and orthodoxy, and limits its action to controlling
and regulating human conduct from a merely 'political'
point of view. This may be so in the modern state, which
is founded upon the admission of freedom of religious
belief and organization. It is certainly not the case with
the Marsilian state. For the Marsilian legislator, with his
pretension to regulate all those aspects of religious life, as
the forms of worship, of church discipline and ecclesiastical
hierarchy, which, though apparently 'external', are far
from being irrelevant to a truly religious conscience, must
defy the fundamental aspirations, that is, the liberty, of
conscience itself. Nor is this all. For indeed in a state
like the one which is described by Marsilius, and which
is grounded on the premiss of religious unity and orthodoxy, religious conformity necessarily becomes a token of
political allegiance. Not only is there no place for religious freedom, but religion itself is debased to a merely
political instrument. It might almost be Machiavelli's conception of religion as *instrumentum regni*; it certainly was
a very dangerous contribution, a truly *damnosa hereditas*,
handed down from medieval thought to later writers.
These writers, as we shall see, were to make full use of the
Marsilian argument, that it is the right of the state,
though professing to aim at a merely 'external' regulation
of human conduct, to exact conformity to the 'established'

religion, and, if necessary, to recur to open persecution of dissent. It is thus to the problem of that contribution that we must return, if we are to conclude this long but, I hope, not too tedious discussion.

Against the older interpretation of Marsilius's doctrine as a striking and somewhat paradoxical anticipation of the future, modern historical criticism has emphasized its transitional character, which is the character of his age. Professor Scholz has repeatedly drawn attention to the fact that the *Defensor Pacis* is the product of an age of transition and crisis, of deep-going transformation in the structure of European social and political life. It is this transformation which affords an explanation of the fact that the germs of later developments are so clearly contained in Marsilius's work. My own contention is, however, that we cannot value this character of transition unless we are fully aware of the traditional elements which are contained in Marsilius's doctrine, and which are reflected in the very issues to which his theory purports to be an answer.

Nowhere perhaps is this double aspect of Marsilius's thought better apparent than in his treatment of that idea which, as I have pointed out already, is a traditional source of inspiration to the medieval mind, but receives an entirely new and surprising treatment at the hands of Marsilius: the idea of unity. No doubt there still is in Marsilius's handling of this idea much which reminds us of the medieval homage to the *ordinatio ad unum*. But, as should appear from what has been said so far, and as appears more fully in chapter xvii of *Defensor Pacis*, Part I, it is quite clear that the principle itself is narrowed down from that essentially metaphysical character which it assumes in St. Thomas and Dante, to one with very particular and new implications: for it is as a deduction from the principle of unity that Marsilius introduces us to that idea of the unitary state which, as Professor Previté-Orton has emphasized, and as I have tried to point out, is the main issue of his discussion. The ultimate absorption of all duality or multiplicity into a mystical unity, which had contented St. Thomas, was to the sceptical and practically minded Marsilius more like a bad joke. His notion of unity comes in fact very near to that notion of sovereignty which is usually conceived to be the mark of modern political thought. His clear grasp of the notion is apparent in the assertion that, whatever the form of government and however divided the supreme power may be in many hands, sovereignty must be conceived as a unit: 'hii plures —the rulers in an aristocracy or democracy—sunt unus principatus numero quantum ad officium'.[1] It appears also in his contention that jurisdiction must have a unique source, 'ne principatuum pluralitate inordinata politiam solvi contingat',[2] and that no other law can be allowed in the state except that of the state itself. And yet this principle was to Marsilius more than that merely legal principle of sovereignty which Bodin was to discover and expound. Marsilius's 'absolutism' is of a very different kind from the modern. It admits of no limitation whatever. His 'sovereign' is not bound by the law of nature, and freely disposes of the law of God. The law of the state is in itself an embodiment of justice. This is not Bodin, but rather Rousseau or Hegel. Obviously enough it is nothing of the sort, but perhaps only the extreme and paradoxical development of some medieval currents of ideas which have not yet been fully retraced and studied. It is here that the problem of the sources of Marsilius's thought

[1] *Defensor Pacis*, I, xvii, § 2.   [2] *Ibid.*, II, viii, § 9.

becomes important; for clearly it is only through a full knowledge of them that the significance of Marsilius's doctrine in the contribution of the Middle Ages to political thought can be adequately valued.

Unfortunately when we come to this, we are left to conjecture. The indebtedness of Marsilius to a particular and well-defined philosophical or theological teaching has not yet been proved conclusively, although much labour has been spent on the subject. The derivation of particular ideas has been disclosed, but the general inspiration of his thought is still in doubt. The two currents of thought which are usually mentioned in discussing this problem are Averroism and Nominalism, those two sides of medieval thought which represent, for different if not opposite reasons, its extreme wings, and are the elements most disruptive of the great scholastic systematization.

The nominalistic influence is subject to serious doubts. It has been pointed out that it was Marsilius who influenced William of Ockham rather than vice versa. And yet there is an undoubtedly nominalistic flavour in Marsilius's theory of law. Marsilius, as we have seen, was a radical and coherent voluntarist. His insistence that will and not reason is the constituent element of law is subversive of the Thomist hierarchies, and is perhaps one of the deepest sources of inspiration for his political theory.

The Averroistic influence is generally admitted and emphasized. There can be little doubt of Marsilius's connexion with Averroistic circles, both in Padua and in Paris, even though scholars no longer allow to the notorious Averroist, John of Jandun, a direct share in the composition of the *Defensor Pacis*. This influence probably accounts for that form of religious scepticism, of which we have seen so many instances in the *Defensor Pacis*, the fruit of a philosophical doctrine which, in Mr. Gilson's words, amounted practically to 'une forme savante d'incrédulité religieuse'.

But the decisive influence on Marsilius's thought is clearly that of Aristotle. It was the revival of the Aristotelian conception of the state which, as Gierke puts it, broke the shell of traditional medieval political thought, or rather, I would say, finds in Marsilius's work an entirely different development from that which it had received in the careful and balanced Thomist adaptation. No doubt there is much in Marsilius's interpretation which seems to correspond to that secularization and humanization (I apologize for the use of such barbarous expressions!) which is usually conceived to be the mark of later political theory. But the very adaptation and distortion of the Aristotelian teaching, its hybrid combination with typically medieval premisses, the very limitation of Marsilius's outlook, are the mark of an age and of a frame of mind which are very remote from our own. Let us therefore not be duped by the apparently 'modern' character of the Marsilian conception of the state and of the ultimate significance and end of human life. Fortunately for us, modern political thought has known of different sources of inspiration. The Marsilian state remains as an illustration of what the state might have been if, besides the Aristotelian influence, other and vital motives had not been contained in the legacy of medieval political thought, if new ideas and forces had not grown up from the very core of our Christian civilization to limit and neutralize the pretence of the state to embody the ultimate value of human life. From this standpoint indeed Marsilius can only appear to us, as he is, a product of his age, a medieval Aristotelian, even though 'homo Aristotelicus magis quam Christianus'.

V

THE AGE OF TRANSMISSION

THE choice of Hooker as an illustration of medieval
political ideas may well appear at first sight somewhat paradoxical. Hooker's name, which to every cultured
Englishman is a symbol of Anglican piety and of beauti-
ful Elizabethan prose, has only of late become familiar
to the historian of political thought, and begun to be
better known also outside England. He almost completely escaped the notice of such careful and widely
read historians as Gierke and Troeltsch. And even in
England the import and meaning of Hooker's political
theory are far from being cleared of all ambiguity. The
teaching of 'that learned and judicious divine' has in fact
been closely bound up in this country with party polemics,
and the very fate of Hooker's work has depended on them.
The publication of the last three books of the *Laws of
Ecclesiastical Polity* long after Hooker's death, as a weapon
of ecclesiastical and political controversy, and the doubts
as to the authenticity of these books which ensued, have
greatly hampered an exact valuation of Hooker's position.
The long-debated question has now, however, been almost
definitely settled in favour of the authenticity of the whole
work, and we can therefore base a discussion of Hooker's
political theory on the whole eight books, the coherence
of whose doctrine throughout had already been pointed
out by Baxter at the height of the seventeenth-century
controversy.[1] Hooker is undoubtedly one of the greatest
systematic thinkers of his age, and like all really great
thinkers, a Janus-like figure, facing two different if not

[1] *A Christian Directory* (1673), in *Works*, ed. Orme, 1830, vol. vi, p. 3.

opposite worlds. Towards the close of a century of controversy, Hooker's work marks the renewal of constructive thought. Hooker's merit lies in having raised a purely
polemical question, as that of the organization of a Protestant church in England, to the level of general principles: and thus his work brings us back to those contrasts
which are ideal and eternal, the contrast between tradition
and radicalism, between reason and faith. It is on this
higher plane that Hooker set himself the task of rebuilding
into a coherent system the main problems of ethics: hence
his elaborate theory of laws, which is in some sense the
key to his discussion of religion and politics, and the condition of a clear understanding of his philosophical standpoint. Hooker's work may thus be compared with that of
the great systematic thinkers of the Middle Ages, like
Thomas Aquinas, whose influence on the outlines of
Hooker's theory has often been pointed out. On the other
hand, the peaceful and lofty sentences of the *Ecclesiastical
Polity* almost invariably contain an answer to the burning
questions started during the Renaissance and the Reformation, and sometimes contain also the germs of doctrines
which were to attain far-reaching developments in later
days. It has been said many times that the greatness of
Hooker is not to be sought in daring novelty or in boldness of thought, but in his admirably clear comprehension
of the great classical and Christian tradition, in the skill
with which he avoided extreme solutions and followed that
via media which has become the ideal and symbol of
Anglicanism and has so greatly contributed to shape the
particular bent of the English mind.

It is for all these reasons that I venture to think
that Hooker's work provides an excellent standpoint for
visualizing the contribution of medieval political thought

to that of modern times and appreciating one aspect of what Dr. Carlyle has recently called the 'continuity of political civilization'. Let me, however, emphasize the fact that such continuity must not be conceived in an exterior and mechanical manner. It is not a question of the mere repetition of certain principles or formulae which continued to remain commonplaces of political discussion long after the close of the Middle Ages. It is a question of the continuity and permanence of certain issues, and of a particular attitude towards the fundamental problems of morals and politics. The continuity of such an attitude, and of the efforts to solve the issues which it implies, are the real test of the continuity of Western political civilization; and historical reconstructions such as those of Troeltsch or Carlyle have conclusively shown that this continuity was only shaken but not broken by the great spiritual and social upheaval of the sixteenth century. It is this fundamental attitude which must always be borne in mind if we are not to misconstrue the apparently paradoxical fact of the repetition, at the hands both of Protestant and of Catholic writers, of traditional slogans, and the real break in the continuity of European political thought, which was the work of truly revolutionary thinkers such as Machiavelli or Hobbes.

In the great effort to provide a satisfactory answer to the problem of political obligation, no conception had been of such value to medieval political thinkers as that of natural law. It is in relation to this conception that the importance of Hooker's position can best be valued. But to understand that position adequately it may be useful to bear in mind some particular aspects of the development of the theory of natural law in England before and during the Reformation.

It has been said that the doctrine of the law of nature was not very successful in England, and the sentence of a glossator of Bracton, 'In Anglia minus curatur de iure naturali quam in aliqua regione de mundo', is often quoted. However this may be, the treatment of the theory of the law of nature by some fifteenth- and sixteenth-century writers affords a good illustration of how the problem of law was viewed by theologians and lawyers on the eve of the Reformation.

The doctrine of the law of nature plays an important part in the works of two very different writers of the fifteenth century, Bishop Pecock and Sir John Fortescue. The latter emphatically reasserts the orthodox theory stated by Aquinas in the *Summa Theologica*. Natural law is that understanding of eternal justice which man can reach through the exercise of his *recta ratio*; its function is one of mediation, as a *luminare minus* which guides us in the affairs of this lower world; all human laws are subordinate to its authority.[1] Starting from the same premisses, Reginald Pecock pushes the identity between the law of nature and reason to its most extreme consequences, thus taking, towards the close of the Middle Ages, a position of advanced rationalism which is of extraordinary interest. In opposition to the Lollards, who maintained the absolute supremacy of the divine law as embodied in the Scripture, and who made the Bible the source and pattern of all laws, Pecock goes to the opposite extreme and exalts the *law of kinde*, which is nothing else than the *doom of reason*, as the independent foundation of morality, over and above the revealed law.[2] The views of both Pecock

[1] Sir John Fortescue, *De Natura Legis Naturae*, c. 1461–3, modern edition by Lord Clermont, 1869: chapters v, xxxi ff., xlii.

[2] Reginald Pecock, *The Repressor of overmuch blaming of the Clergy*, c. 1450, modern edition by Ch. Babington, Rolls Series, 1860.

and his opponents are extreme ones: orthodox medieval doctrine steered a middle course in the endeavour to reconcile harmoniously the *lex naturalis* and the *lex divina*, the sphere of human reason with that of supernatural truth.

One might expect that the shrewd reaction against scholasticism, which characterizes the influence of Humanism and the Renaissance and is openly proclaimed by the Oxford Reformers, would have marked the abandonment of the old theory of the law of nature. But the Renaissance could not but foster the belief in the reasonable nature of man as a guide to perfection. The inhabitants of Utopia 'define vertue to be life ordered according to nature and that we be hereunto ordeined of God. And that he dothe followe the course of nature, which in desiering and refusinge thinges is ruled by reason'.[1] This is enough, I think, to show in More a clear grasp of the idea of the law of nature, and More himself is careful and orthodox to the point of adding that besides the rule of reason, a higher way to perfection may be revealed to man from heaven. The belief in the harmony between the laws of nature and the principles of the Christian religion is, as Seebohm pointed out, one of the strongholds of the Oxford Reformers; and it is interesting to hear in More's own words what he conceived to be the relation between reason and faith, and what he thought of Luther's discrediting of reason: 'And so must reason not resist faith but walk with her, and as her handmaid so wait upon her, that as contrary as ye take her, yet of a truth faith goeth never without her.... And therefore are in mine opinion these Lutherans in a mad mind that would now have all learning save Scripture only clean cast away....'[2]

---

[1] Sir Thomas More, *Utopia*, translation of Raphe Robinson, second book, 'Of their journeying or travayling abrode', &c.

[2] *Dialogue concerning Tyndale*, ed. by W. E. Campbell, 1927, pp. 86–7.

It is especially from the lawyers that we might expect open and frequent talk about natural law. But the principal vehicle of the doctrine of the law of nature was canon law, and this connexion doomed it to unpopularity among English laymen. This may afford an explanation of a famous passage by the greatest English lawyer of the first half of the sixteenth century, Christopher Saint-German:

'It is not used among them that be learned in the laws of England to reason what thing is commanded or prohibited by the law of nature, and what not, but all the reasoning in that behalf is under this manner. As when any thing is grounded upon the law of nature, they say, that reason will that such a thing be done; and if it be prohibited by the law of nature, they say it is against reason, or that reason will not suffer that to be done'.[1]

But if this passage is a statement of the diffidence of English lawyers in regard to the abstract constructions of natural law, it is also a frank recognition of the necessities in view of which the theory of natural law is devised, and evidence of the identity of the conclusions reached under the cover of 'reason' or of 'nature'. In fact, when he comes to classify and define the several kinds of laws, Saint-German has no hesitation in borrowing wholesale from the schoolmen, and the framework of his system of the laws of England is a theory of the law of nature which comes very near to the theories of Aquinas and Gerson. Saint-German's work, as Vinogradoff has pointed out, is an attempt to justify the body of English law in name of its reasonableness, and it contains the very important recognition that the principles of reason are not necessarily universal and abstract, but may be drawn from historical growth. We shall see how this idea, which has become a lasting inherit-

---

[1] Christopher Saint-German, *Doctor and Student, or Dialogues between a Doctor of Divinity and a Student in the Laws of England*; Latin, 1523, English, 1530–1; modern edition, Cincinnati, 1886.

ance not only of English legal tradition, but of the English mind, is fully developed by Hooker.

The different theories which I have summarized are instances of the different manner in which the traditional doctrine of natural law was capable of developing without losing its fundamental character. The law of nature is the key to the system of laws, leading down from the law of God to the human laws of particular states.

To understand the change which this doctrine underwent in the Reformation is of very great importance to the historian of political philosophy. In his *Social Teaching of the Christian Churches*, Troeltsch, as is well known, has tried to show the thorough transformation of the old idea through the influence of Protestant theology. The emphasis on the corruption of human nature and the absolute sovereignty of God led to a new conception of the standard of justice, embodied in a new idea of the law of nature. It is, according to Troeltsch, this new idea of the law of nature which explains the deep change of attitude towards social and political problems, which was the outcome of Protestantism. But it has, on the other hand, been maintained that the whole conception of natural law, conceived as a mediatory element between God and man and a defence of the power and dignity of human nature, was out of place, and actually found very little room, in the Reformers' theology. The Reformation, it is said, brings to fulfilment the work of Nominalism, in utterly destroying the hierarchical conception of the world and supplanting reason by will as the foundation of ethics; hence its insistence upon Scripture, the revealed law of God, as the sole rule of human action; hence its distrust of the whole mass of rational arguments embodied in the law of nature. The writers who deny Troeltsch's main thesis are thus brought to maintain that a direct result of Protestantism in the field of political theory was the comparative disparagement of natural law in favour of the divine law embodied in the Bible, and of the positive law of the state conceived as ultimately grounded upon the will of God.

The question thus abstractly set out may seem one of words, and yet undoubtedly momentous consequences are involved in its solution; for on it depends an understanding of the process by which human thought was severed from the grip of a dogmatic age, and political theory became secularized. The difficulties in which the writers who have discussed the question have become entangled are due in a large measure to the abstract and schematic form which they have adopted. Troeltsch's theory of a Christian natural law was mainly devised to illustrate the variations of moral and political standards in the course of the development of Christian ethics, and it enabled him to give a brilliant synthesis of the relations between religious ideals and political theory. Yet it is undoubtedly true that among the first effects of the Reformation upon political theory was the forsaking of the rational arguments of natural law, and of any systematic treatment of the highest problems of law and politics. Thus the law of the Bible and the law of the state were left as the main if not the only ground of controversy. I shall limit my inquiry into the history of natural law during this crisis to England, where the question has not yet received the attention it deserves, and where the problems and solutions of the Reformation are in many ways greatly different from those of the Continent.

If, as may be argued, the first stage of the Reformation in England, which centres round the Caesaro-papistical experiment of Henry VIII, did not bring forth any

particularly new idea in the field of political theory, one of
its results was to give a tragical actuality to one problem,
which the traditional theory of law had attempted to solve:
the problem of the conflict of laws. Positive law was confronted with positive law, divine right opposed to divine
right. Over and against the positive law of a universal
church, claiming universal allegiance, the positive law of
one particular kingdom with a growing consciousness of
national independence was asserted. It is not our task here
to examine whether and how effectively the clash between the two systems of law had been foreshadowed in
medieval England, nor to determine how much of Henry's
proceedings could be supported with the old rusty weapons
against Rome, or had to be enforced as a startling and
unheard-of innovation. But however valid a support precedent and enactment could offer, positive law does not provide a much better foundation for a right than does mere
force. A higher, and, according to the times, a more unquestionable, argument had to be found, to invest the new-born
national sovereignty with that religious halo which, for the
time being, seemed the only possible ground of unconditional allegiance. That halo was provided by divine right.

Professor Allen has pointed out that the early Tudor
monarchy sorely needed a doctrine of the religious duty
of obedience to constituted authority, but he is at pains
to show that the doctrine required and taught was not
anything that could actually be called a theory of the
divine right of kings. This is undoubtedly true as far
as concerns that completely elaborated theory of divine
right and of the excellence of legitimate and irresponsible
monarchy, which was to characterize Stuart and Bourbon
autocracy. The doctrine of obedience was certainly, as
Professor Allen emphasizes, the real pivot of Tudor poli-

tical theory, and the strength of the English conviction of
the wickedness of rebellion is to be attributed much less
to religion or to any theory of divine right than to immediate expediency and to the growth of patriotic sentiment.

But whatever may have been the immediate necessities
concealed behind the resounding phrase, the claim of
divine right appears as the favourite argument of the
defenders of Henry VIII, and as their main ground in
proclaiming the duty of allegiance. Hints of a different
kind of argument in favour of the supremacy of the
national sovereign over state and church are not wanting,
and we shall estimate further on their importance and
trace their development in later English political theory;
but indeed the almost tiresome repetition of the appeal to
the *jus divinum* (the power of the King has to be obeyed
because so God commands) is the best proof of the absence
of any speculation upon the origin and nature of political
authority. It appears as if the subjugation of the church
and the foundation of the modern state as 'one body
politic living under the allegiance of the King as supreme
imperial head and sovereign'[1] could not be effected except
by turning against the usurped jurisdiction of the bishop
of Rome those very weapons which had served to establish its power. Had not, as late as 1515, Wolsey, kneeling
before the King, pleaded the law of God in defence of
clerical immunities? It was not enough to oppose the
positive law of the King to the canon law of the Popes,
and to make sure that the power of enforcing obedience
lay altogether in the hands of the sovereign; it was not
enough to have learnt the lesson of the *plenitudo potestatis*
and of the monstrousness of a two-headed body; the final

---

[1] *Draft*, corrected by Cromwell, in *Letters and Papers*, Henry VIII, vol. v,
1880, n. 721, p. 343.

argument of papal supporters had to be expunged, divine right denied to the Pope and vindicated on behalf of the King. Thus we see Henrician pamphleteers all at one in contrasting the claim of the King as grounded upon the law of God with the merely human right of the bishop of Rome.[1] It should be noticed of these antipapal writers that while some, like Fox or Sampson, showed no interest at all in the new religious opinions, others, like Gardiner, were at pains to save their theological orthodoxy from an unwelcome situation. It is very important that some of them, Gardiner for instance, when returning in later days to the fold of the Roman church, should at least on this point have maintained a certain consistency; Gardiner, according to M. Janelle, could never be brought to see in the Papacy more than a purely human institution. Thus in the terrible straits into which their King and Sovereign Lord had brought them, the only means of escape which high officials of the church and religious conservatives could find was to lay down clearly, born casuists as they were, the terms of the conflict as a conflict of laws. When they had decided that 'divine right' fully turned the scale in favour of the King, they could think their conscience at peace.

But others might not or could not accept this happy

---

[1] This is the main argument of contemporary writers. Cp. Christopher Saint-German, *Salem and Bizance*, London, Berthelet, 1533; Richard Sampson, *Oratio qua docet, hortatur, admonet omnes . . . Anglos, regiae dignitati cum primis ut obediant*, London, Berthelet, 1533; the *Opus eximium de vera differentia Regiae potestatis et ecclesiasticae*, probably by Edward Fox or Foxe, London, Berthelet, 1534. The argument also recurs in Stephen Gardiner's sermon *On true obedience* (Latin, 1536; English, 1553; modern edition by P. Janelle, 1930); in John Bekinsau's treatise *De Supremo et absoluto Regis Imperio*, London, Berthelet, 1547; and both in the *Bishop's Book* (*The Institution of a Christian Man*, 1537) and the *King's Book* (*A necessary Doctrine and Erudition for any Christen Man*, 1543. The name of *King's Book* was also given sometimes to Foxe's *De vera differentia*).

solution. St. Thomas More may be taken as the pathetic illustration of the tragical debate. It seems almost as if the issue had already been foreshadowed in *Utopia*. It is, as Professor Chambers admirably puts it,[1] the issue 'between the men who merely obey the laws of the state, and the men who have, as every citizen of Utopia was bound to have, a belief that there is an ultimate standard of right and wrong, beyond what the state may at any moment command'. And now the moment had come. More had put the case before his conscience and decided. 'Diligent examination' had shown him that one particular realm, 'being but a member and small part of the church, might not make a particular law disagreeable to the general law of Christ's universal Catholic Church, no more than the city of London, being but one poor member in respect of the whole realm, might make a law against an Act of Parliament to bind the whole realm'. Hence a positive law directly repugnant to the laws of God and His holy Church could not and should not be obeyed, even if martyrdom were the issue. 'I am not bounden, my Lord, to conform my conscience to the Council of one realm, against the general Council of Christendom.'

If we turn to those writers who were not primarily involved in the defence of Henry VIII's Byzantinism, but whose main concern was religious reformation and the establishment of the newly discovered Gospel truth, we find that an even greater emphasis, though of a different kind, was laid upon divine law. The pioneers of Protestant doctrine in England extol, as the Lollards had done, the absolute supremacy of the word of God as revealed in Scripture, and at the same time insist upon its purely spiritual character: hence they show a comparative

[1] *Thomas More*, London, 5th ed., 1936, p. 398.

indifference to human affairs and to political conditions. There is little room left, in the radical antinomy of human and divine law, for the old *lex naturae*, which had brought heaven and earth into harmony and raised the human creature to the dignity of a lawgiver and a judge. 'A Christian man, in respect of God, is but a passive thing,' says Tyndale, and must therefore bow his head to whatever God allows to happen in this weary world. Power is granted to Princes, even to evil ones, by God, and unlimited bodily subjection is the counterpart of the spiritual liberty of the Christian.[1] Passive obedience is the sum of the early Reformers' political theory, if they had any at all; no wonder that Henry was as quick to take up the priceless suggestion as he was ready to allow its authors to be burnt on the charge of heresy.

We might expect the idea of natural law to play a prominent part when it became necessary to elaborate a theory of resistance. This happened, as with continental Protestantism, only under the pressure of circumstances. The first preachers of the Reformation in England had made it a strong point that theirs should be a doctrine of obedience, while the Papists not only admitted but openly proclaimed the right and duty of active resistance.[2] The medieval and Catholic theory of resistance had found its solid ground in the theory of natural law. Scriptural precedents and constitutional proceedings may show the way and provide the means for active resistance; but its main foundation lies in

---

[1] Robert Barnes, *That mens constitutions, which are not grounded in Scripture, bynde not the conscience of man under the payne of deadly sinne* (in Foxe's Collection, *The whole works of W. Tyndale, John Frith and Doct. Barnes*, London, 1573); William Tyndale, *The obedience of a christian man*, 1528 (ed. by R. Lovett, London, 1888).

[2] Robert Barnes, *A Supplication unto the most gracious Prince King Henry VIII*, 1534 (in Foxe's Collection, noted above).

the rational character of political obligation, and it is the law of nature, embodying the principles of human justice, which sets the conditions and limits of obedience. If the Marian exiles, to whom fell the task of constructing a doctrine of resistance, do not appear to have made much use of the easy and simple traditional doctrine, this may be attributed to theological objections and distrust of rational argumentation, as well as to hesitation on their part in forsaking so completely what had been one of the main points of early Protestant teaching. Their appeal to the natural law is mingled with and ultimately submerged in a completely different sort of argumentation: the appeal to Scripture and to constitutional rules. The interesting point in these writings, especially in Poynet's *Shorte Treatise of politike power*, is the appeal to the actual facts (or to what Poynet believed to be the actual facts) of the English Constitution.[1] But the predominant and favourite argument remained the appeal to the will of God, unmistakably set forth in Scripture. The small part which was left to the law of nature would be hardly worth mentioning were it not to illustrate how confused and inadequate the theory had become.[2]

Thus by the time that England with the advent of Elizabeth was definitely binding up her course with that of Protestantism, the *jus divinum*, the word of God revealed in the Bible, seemed to have become with theologians the final argument even on the subject of politics:

[1] This constitutional bias of the Protestant theory of resistance was strongly stressed by later Anglican divines. Cp. John Jewel, *A defence of the Apologie*, in *Works*, Parker Society, vol. iii, Cambridge, 1848, p. 172; and especially Thomas Bilson, *The true difference between christian subjection and unchristian Rebellion*, Oxford, 1585, pp. 508–18.

[2] John Poynet, *Shorte Treatise of politike power* (n.p., but probably Strasbourg, 1556; reprint, 1639); Christopher Goodman, *How Superior Powers ought to be obeyed of their subjects*, Geneva, 1558.

they had managed to find in it their political creed, and
to invoke it in turn for support of passive obedience and
of active resistance. The counterpart to this ingenuous
biblicalism is the unprejudiced and worldly realism with
which laymen begin to look at the problem of politics.
Machiavelli's teaching, it seems, was beginning to bear its
fruits. Lawyers and politicians began to think of the state
and of positive law in terms of mere force. They drew
their lesson from the 'new polity' inaugurated by Henry
VIII, upon which—in Pollard's words—the 'ship of the
state' had started 'on its piratical cruise into the uncharted
seas of self-determination'. From the point of view of
political theory, their grasp of the idea of sovereignty is
of the greatest importance; their insight into the tech-
nique of government and the mutability of its rules is
also significant in many ways; but the problem of justice
and of political obligation does not appear to have given
them much trouble. Sir Thomas Smith, writing in 1565,
went indeed so far as to acknowledge some truth in the
contention of Thrasimachus in Plato's *Republic*, that the
highest standard of justice in a city or commonwealth is
the convenience of the ruling part.[1]

The merit of bringing the problem of political obligation again into the foreground, and of restoring speculation
tion about the state to its ancient and proper terms, as the
product of human activities which has to be justified less
through divine sanction or brutal force than through the
rational character of human nature, belongs to a generation whose main task was to reconcile the old tradition of
learning with the achievements of the Reformation. This
is the generation which reconstructed the English Church

---

[1] Sir Thomas Smith, *De Republica Anglorum*, 1565, published in 1583: modern
edition by Alston, Cambridge, 1906; book I, chs. 1–2.

and gave it a lasting foundation. I am not here directly concerned with the dogmatical and theological issues of the
Elizabethan settlement. The ambiguity with which they
were defined is, and will probably remain for ever, a crucial
problem. But the very carefulness with which extreme
doctrinal standpoints were avoided was to set its mark
upon the subsequent life of the Church of England. The
bias of its early divines for advanced Protestant views
mattered in the end much less than their humanistic train-
ing, their aversion to radicalism of any kind, their endeavour
to reconstruct unity upon a broader basis. A deep sense
of the historical and social aspect of religion, a distrust
of individual opinions, and hence a clear-cut distinction
between the spheres of divine and of human authority:
these are the main features of Anglican thought and also
its peculiar contribution to political theory.

The futility of appealing to Scripture as a guide in
political matters, and the insufficiency of mere *jus
divinum* as a standard for secular life, are clearly enun-
ciated by Anglican loyalists at the accession of Elizabeth.
Goodman and Knox had proclaimed on scriptural grounds
the unlawfulness of the government of women, and the
invalidity of succession inconsistent with the law of
God.[1] To this Aylmer replied: 'I must say this to them
all in general, that the Scripture meddleth with no civil
policy further than to teach obedience. And therefore
whatsoever is brought out of the Scripture concerning
any kind of regiment, is without the booke, pulled into
the game place by the eares to wrastle whether it will
or not. For Christ saith: *Quis me constituit inter vos*

---

[1] Christopher Goodman, *How Superior Powers ought to be obeyed* (as above);
John Knox, *The First Blast of the Trumpet against the Monstrous Regiment of
Women*, 1558, in *Works*, ed. Laing, vol. iv.

judicem? Who hath made me betwixt you a judge? As
though he should say, myne office is not to determyne
matters of pollicy, of succession, and enheritaunce, for
that belongeth to the civill magistrates.'[1] This passage
is very interesting both because of the time at which it
was written and for its implications. If divine law does
not provide any available ground for the solution of
political problems, some other ground must be found
for the justification of civil power and for the construction of political theory.

But it is characteristic of an age which was still at
bottom theologically minded, that it was a controversy
upon religious and ecclesiastical matters which once more
made the whole problem of law and politics the object of
careful and adequate examination. The Puritan attack on
the established church was certainly one in which political
questions, as well as those of religion and church policy,
were involved. And the political implications of their
doctrines, as their first great opponent was quick to detect,
were from the beginning dangerous to the Elizabethan
state.[2] Yet the Puritan challenge to the church of
England was primarily and essentially the challenge of
a narrow and intolerant scripturalism to every human
authority and to all historical development. 'That nothing
be don in this or any other thing, but that which you have
the expresse warrante of God's Worde for' was the principle laid down in the first Puritan manifesto.[3] This biblical

---

[1] John Aylmer, *An Harborowe for faithfull and trewe subiectes*, Strasbourg,
1559. There is a close correspondence between the Anglican teaching and that
of the Zürich divines, such as Bullinger, which appears also in other points; see
below, p. 138.

[2] John Whitgift, *Works*, ed. for the Parker Society by J. Ayre, ii. 239–64.

[3] *First Admonition to Parliament*, 1571/2, in *Puritan Manifestoes*, ed. by Frere
and Douglas, London, 1907.

radicalism, which is not unlike that which the Lollards had professed, implied the sweeping away of the whole mass of traditions, doctrines, and ordinances which had arisen with time and upon which the church of England, reformed but Catholic, still rested. I am not here concerned with the several arguments with which the defenders of the English church tried to meet the Puritan challenge. It is enough to notice that, as Mr. Usher has remarked, Whitgift, the formidable Bancroft, and all the minor apologists of the church, had either met the Puritans upon their own ground, Scripture, or appealed to reasons of convenience and policy. No doubt much stress was laid by Whitgift upon the value of man's reason and experience, which in his hands became a strong argument against the infallibility both of Pope and of Scripture; and it is important to note that the claim of the Presbytery to possess a *jus divinum* was not, so far, met with a mere *jure divino* counterclaim in favour of the episcopal government of the church.[1] But it is the greatness of Hooker to have raised the discussion to a higher plane and to have laid bare its real issues: to do this a theological independence was required which Whitgift, still under the spell of Calvin's theology, did not possess. It was necessary to go back to those fundamental problems upon which the general outlook on the world depended. It was thus with a thorough-going re-examination of the problem of law that Hooker started on his defence of the laws of the church of England.

'Our largeness of speech how men do find out what things reason bindeth them of necessity to observe, and what it guideth them to

---

[1] Whitgift, *Works*, i. 6 and 183, 191: cp. R. G. Usher, *The supposed origin of the divine right of the Bishops*, in *Mélanges d'histoire offerts à M. Charles Bémont*, 1913.

choose in things which are left as arbitrary; the care we have had
to declare the different nature of laws which severally concern all
men, from such as belong to men either civilly or spiritually associated, such as pertain to the fellowship which nations, or which
Christian nations, have amongst themselves, and in the last place
such as concerning every or any of these God himself hath revealed
by his Holy Word: all serveth but to make manifest, that as the
actions of men are of sundry distinct kinds, so the laws thereof must
accordingly be distinguished. There are in men operations, some
natural, some rational, some supernatural, some politic, some finally
ecclesiastical: which if we measure not each by his own proper law,
whereas the things themselves are so different, there will be in our
understanding and judgment of them confusion.'[1]

'They hold that one only law, the Scripture, must be
the rule to direct in all things, even so far—the blow is
directed at Cartwright—as to the "taking up of a rush or
straw".'[2] To show the narrowness and danger of such a
creed, Hooker used all the resources of his eloquence and
humour. It is both the negative and the constructive
application of the principle which he attacks. In the Preface, where the argument against fanaticism is *ad hominem*,
and the Puritan, as Dr. Scott-Pearson would say, is 'psycho-
analysed' through and through, Hooker tells an instruc-
tive story about a set of fanatics—the Anabaptists—who
had claimed to ground themselves upon the exclusive
command of God. Hooker is not content with pointing at
their disastrous example: an argument much used in the
sixteenth century by controversialists of all parties. He
draws attention to the perverted notions upon which they
based their conduct. 'When they and their Bibles were
alone together, what strange fantastical opinion soever at
any time entered into their heads, their use was to think the

[1] Richard Hooker, *Of the Laws of Ecclesiastical Polity*, in *Works*, arranged by
Keble, 7th ed. revised by Church and Paget, Oxford, 1888; I. xvi. 5.
[2] *Eccl. Pol.* II. i. 2.

Spirit taught it them.'[1] The Puritan claim to infallibility
was met by Hooker with a dispassionate analysis of the
nature and grounds of persuasion. Whole sections of the
Ecclesiastical Polity are but enlargements upon this theme,
and the power of Hooker's reasoning is so great that one
is sometimes in danger of forgetting that after all the position of his opponents also contains an element of permanent value: for a great moral force underlies and to a
certain extent justifies the Puritan refusal of compromise
and their rigid assertion of principle.

But Hooker can see no valid ground behind the Puritan's conscientious objection. It is based upon a fundamental mistake, their distrust and disparagement of all
that is human. It amounts to a sceptical denial of all
foundations of certainty. The authority both of reason
and of history is rejected, as if, to make God's glory more
apparent, it was necessary utterly to destroy the dignity of
man. 'The name of the light of nature is made hateful
with men; the "star of reason and learning", and all other
such like helps, beginneth no otherwise to be thought of
than if it were an unlucky comet. . . .'[2]

That Hooker's concern should have been to detect in
the Puritan a bad philosopher is an aspect of his work
which has not been enough considered; and yet, as Dean
Church pointed out, it is the key to his theory of natural
law. It is only after proving the doctrinal errors of the
Puritans that Hooker proceeded to examine their political
implications. With the proper foundations of ethics
firmly established, the remedy to the 'late troubles' was
easy to find: for it was only a question of distinguishing
what had been confused and of once more putting things
in their right perspective. Here again the crucial point is

---

[1] *Eccl. Pol.*, Pref. viii. 7.   [2] *Ibid.* III. viii. 4.

the value and use of the *jus divinum*. For, logically applied, did not the Puritan conception of the *jus divinum* as containing directions for 'whatsoever things can fall into any part of man's life' imply the overthrow of all law not directly reducible to Scripture? As for the Canon Law, the Puritans had long since declared war against it, nor did they spare the Civil Law, disdaining 'the singular treasures of wisdom therein contained'. This attitude if followed out to its logical conclusion ended in complete radicalism.

'The reasons wherewith ye would persuade that Scripture is the only rule to frame all our actions by, are in every respect as effectual for proof that the same is the only law whereby to determine all our civil controversies. And then what doth let, but that as those men may have their desire, who frankly broach it already that the work of reformation will never be perfect, till the law of Jesus Christ be received alone; so pleaders and counsellors may bring their books of the common law, and bestow them as the students of curious and needless arts did theirs in the Apostles' time?'[1]

Again, might not the same kind of reasoning with which the Puritans tried to prove that the laws of church government are contained in Scripture, be equally applied to the laws of the state? Why should God 'less regard our temporal estate in this world, or provide for it worse' than for that of the Jews? Some people indeed think that 'the grafting of the Gentiles and their incorporating into Israel doth import that we ought to be subject unto the rites and laws of their whole polity'.[2] But the Puritans will admit—and again Hooker quotes Cartwright—that God has left us 'at greater liberty in things civil', though of course denying 'the like liberty in things pertaining to the king-

---

[1] *Eccl. Pol.*, Pref. viii. 4; the same point was made in the first answer of the Bishops to the Marprelate Tracts; see Thomas Cooper, *An Admonition to the People of England*, 1589, reprint by E. Arber, 1883, pp. 65–6.

[2] *Ibid.* III. xi. 4.

dom of Heaven'.[1] It is true that the Puritan distinction of
the two kingdoms implied a notion of relativity in all that
concerns the state: as against the immutable uniformity
of God-given church government, civil government is
alterable according to circumstances. This may amount,
as Dr. Scott-Pearson has emphasized, to a denial of any
'divine right' on the side of the state, but, on the other
hand, it does not imply the recognition of even a comparative independence of politics from the supremacy of
the *jus divinum*. For, in Puritan deductions, not only did
this supremacy mean the duty of the civil power to govern
according to the law of God as interpreted by the Presby-
terian church; not only did it imply that the commonwealth must be framed and fashioned in agreement with
the church of God 'as the hanging with the house'; it
practically amounted to the flat denial of any sort of liberty
of the state 'in things civil', the Bible being the mirror of
all laws and the solid ground for an assertion and vindication of imprescriptible rights. It seems almost as if
Hooker were foreseeing the day when the Puritans, on the
strength of their Bible, would challenge the authority and
power of the state, and suffer exile rather than endure any
limitation of their God-given 'rights'. A good illustration
of the case is given in the discussion of holidays. 'Seeing
that . . . the Lord hath left it to all men at liberty that they
may labour if they think good, six days; I say', wrote
Cartwright, 'the church nor no man, can take away this
liberty from them, and drive them to a necessary rest
of the body.'[2] Is this not a vindication of individual

---

[1] *Eccl. Pol.* III. xi. 10.

[2] Thomas Cartwright, in *Whitgift's Works*, ii. 569: also quoted by Hooker
in note to *Eccl. Pol.* v. lxxi. 3. More radical and general claims can be found in
the Separatists; see Robert Browne, *A Treatise of Reformation without tarrying
for anie*, &c., 1582 (modern edition, London, 1903).

rights on the basis of *jus divinum*? 'This doctrine of yours is very licentious', so Whitgift had already answered, 'and tendeth too much to carnal and corporal liberty, and indeed is a very perilous doctrine for all states'.[1] Hooker points out the necessary implications of the principle: 'without some express commandment of God there is no power they say under heaven which may presume by any decree to restrain the liberty that God hath given', and he shows what would be the consequences of its rigid application in any state.[2] It is precisely in the sphere of things indifferent, which 'God doth neither command nor forbid' that, as we shall see, lawful human authority has its power. Hooker defends in this sphere the 'public power of all societies', which extends 'above every soul contained in the same': whether he goes too far and whether that power is extended to things which are not Caesar's is a matter which will call for a close examination.

Finally, by turning to examine the Puritan interpretation of the *jus divinum*, Hooker carried the discussion on to his opponents' territory, and pointed out the inconsistencies of what the Puritans contended to be their solid and unattackable ground. His theory of the mutability of laws applies to the law of God as well as to all other laws. Against the rigid Puritan scripturalism Hooker pleaded for an historical rather than a legal interpretation of the *jus divinum*. It was to him a source of serious 'misconceits' to believe that all laws established by men are mutable, and all laws delivered by God immutable. He will show that on the contrary both human and divine laws are susceptible of alteration according to the matter

---

[1] Whitgift, *Works*, ii, p. 570; cp. also Thomas Cooper's *Admonition*, p. 156. For the Anglican theory of ἀδιάφορα or 'things indifferent' as the proper field of political authority, see below, p. 124.

[2] *Eccl. Pol.* v. lxxi. 3, 4.

and end for which they were made. 'The reason why things were instituted' must in both cases be considered, and right reason here also be the guide of our judgments. But if the Puritans err in their interpretation of the law of God, even more do they err when they present, as grounded upon *jus divinum*, what is in fact only grounded upon their own particular representation. This amazing weakness in Puritan thought had been seized upon readily by Anglican writers, who pointed out that much of the Puritan 'platform', which ought to have been founded upon Scripture, was in reality only 'the product of men's brains'.[1] Dr. Scott Pearson has lately come to much the same conclusion. The Puritans, he remarks, professed to find their ideas in Scripture, but they frequently found there just what they sought; their belief was based as much upon reason as upon the express word of God, or more exactly upon revelation as interpreted by their own rational preconceptions. Hooker's contention is that all the Puritan's errors proceeded from their erroneous notion of the hierarchy of laws. In all their appeal to Scripture they were doing no more than follow 'the law of private reason, where the law of public should take place'.[2] Hooker's theory of law is primarily intended to put things in their right order again.

In Dean Church's words, the key to Hooker's theory of law is the idea of the concurrence and co-operation of several authorities in the directing of human life: the authority of faith and of reason, of individual persuasion and of general agreement. The necessity of opposing the challenge of scriptural radicalism and of vindicating a sphere of

[1] John Bridges, *A defence of the government established in the Church of England for ecclesiastical matters*, London, 1587, p. 13; Richard Bancroft, *A Sermon preached at Paules Cross*, London, 1588/9.

[2] *Eccl. Pol.* I. xvi. 6.

purely human concern accounts for the large part which
is played in Hooker's defence of the *Laws of Ecclesiastical
Polity* by the idea of natural law: as Lang has put it, 'the
uncompromising *jus divinum* called the *jus naturae* with a
certain necessity into the arena'. But the return to the idea
of natural law necessarily implied the restoration of a
tradition of thought which had for a time been interrupted.
It is here therefore that we must look for an explanation of
Hooker's attitude, and of his deliberate return to the teaching of the Schoolmen. His judgement of the value of
scholastic doctrine is a positive one. Scotus was to him 'the
wittiest of the School-divines', with whose teaching on the
most abstruse and difficult question of God's justice he
'confesses' himself in agreement. Thomas Aquinas is 'the
greatest among the School-divines', whose theories, when
inacceptable, are explained away as 'but a little overflowing
of wit'. This clearly indicates a very different temper from
that which had 'sette Duns in Bocardo' and had turned
the name of the wittiest Schoolman into the ignominious
appellation of fools.[1] Hooker may not have been himself
perfectly conscious of the implications which the modern
reader detects behind even the index of his sources. He
certainly became aware of them under the stress of circumstances.

There is a remarkable difference of tone between
Hooker's earlier and later line of defence in this respect.
He is indeed almost apologetic in his *Answer to Travers*.
'If . . . I used the distinctions and helps of the schools,
I trust that herin I have committed no unlawful thing.
These school-implements are acknowledged by grave and
wise men not unprofitable to have been invented.' Even
Calvin, Hooker points out, had sometimes approved and

---

[1] C. E. Mallet, *A history of the University of Oxford*, vol. ii, 1924, p. 62.

made use of them. 'The most approved for learning and judgment do use them without blame; the use of them hath been well liked in some that have taught even in this very place before me,' &c.[1] In his marginal notes to the Corpus copy of the *Christian Letter*—that priceless document of Hooker's most intimate convictions and the last undoubtedly genuine expression of his thought—Hooker vindicated his position with a very different assurance. The Puritans had unmasked their batteries and there could no longer be any doubt as to what actually was at stake in the discussion. They had contributed to the clearing of the issue by setting upon the same plane the authority of philosophers and the use and value of human reason. 'In all your discourse'—they had accused Hooker —'for the most parte, Aristotle the patriarch of philosophers (with divers other humane writers) and the ingenuous schoolemen, almost in all points have some finger: reason is highlie sett up against Holie Scripture, and reading against preaching.' Hooker's comment upon this charge may well have been written, as Bishop Paget has remarked, with the quiet smile that a contemporary marks as characteristic of him. 'If Aristotle and the Schoolmen be such perilous creatures, you must needes think yourself an happie man, whome God hath so fairely blest from too much knowledg in them.' He jots down some references to be worked out later on: 'Remember heer S. Jerome's Epistle in his own defense. Forget not Picus Mirandula's judgement of the schoolemen—Beza's judgment of Aristotle—as also Calvin's judgment of philosophie.'[2]

Hooker did not live to complete his answer to the

[1] *Hooker's Works*, iii. 586; the *Answer to Travers* goes back to the years of the Temple controversy (1585-6) which was the occasion for the writing of the *Ecclesiastical Polity*.

[2] The *Christian Letter* was published in 1599; the date of Hooker's death is

anonymous Puritan attack. An elaborate reply to it was published three years after his death in Covel's *Just and Temperate Defence*, where one section treats 'of Schoolmen, Philosophie, and Poperye'.[1] Covel, after having endeavoured to explain away Luther's alleged condemnation of scholastic philosophy, distinguishes between the 'scholasticall kinde of expounding' which was used already by the Fathers, and 'the new and later kinde of Schoole interpreting . . . whose methode is Philosophicall disputing, made of Aristotelian learning', and which began 'some foure hundreth and odde years ago'. 'Many that were excellent in this kind', Covel points out, 'the Church both knoweth how to use with great profit, and in recompence of their labour, hath given them titles, with much honour'; among these writers Covel mentions Alexander of Hales, Bonaventure the *Seraphical* doctor, and Aquinas called *Angelical*. 'Now for any man to follow the steps of these, though treading sure, as having more light, can any man in reason account it to be a fault? Is there no other matter of reproofe in Maister Hooker's writings, but that vertues must be faults?' But at this point Covel is aware of the real motives which underlie the Puritan reproof of Hooker's philosophical method, and can find no other reply except by bringing back the question to the essential terms which Hooker had laid bare, and paraphrasing his own words:

'But hee seeketh to prove matters of divinity with the strength of reason: Indeed this is a great fault, which if many had not been

Nov. 2, 1600. Almost all Hooker's annotations were published by Keble; the *Christian Letter* with Hooker's notes are reprinted in R. Bayne's edition of the Fifth Book of the *Ecclesiastical Polity*, 1902.

1 William Covel or Covell, *A Just and Temperate Defence of the five Books of Ecclesiastical Policie: written by M. Richard Hooker: Against an uncharitable Letter of certain English Protestants*, &c., London, 1603.

afraid to commit, the world had not beene filled with so many idle, and unreasonable discourses. But so it is, that through an ignorant zeale of honouring the Scriptures, the name of the light of nature is made hatefull with men; the starre of reason, and learning, and all other such like helps, beginneth no otherwise to be thought of, then as if it were an unlucky Comet, or as if God had so accursed it, that it should never shine, or give light in things, concerning our duty, any way toward Him.'[1]

No doubt there is in Hooker's philosophical standpoint a deep affinity with the traditional ideas which he set himself to defend. His idea of a hierarchical order of the world, expressed in the hierarchy of laws, is essentially congenial to the idea of an ordered and graded society, which is typical of the Elizabethan age. Thus the explanation of the survival of the traditional body of teaching may well lie in the fact that, in Professor Tawney's words, much of the Elizabethan outlook upon life was still medieval rather than modern in its spirit; and of that outlook 'the classical expression, at once the most Catholic, the most reasonable and the most sublime, is the work of Hooker'. Yet when all this is said, the importance of Hooker's effort in defending the inheritance of medieval thought ought not to be undervalued. It is the role of some among the greatest sixteenth- and seventeenth-century thinkers to mark with unquestionable evidence the boundaries between medieval and modern thought. The merits of Hooker will appear to us only if we consider that his whole effort lies in the opposite direction. He endeavoured to gather up the threads of traditional political speculation, the results of centuries of effort and reflection upon the problem of political obligation, and thus restored the theory of law and government to its proper basis, which is a philoso-

[1] *A Just and Temperate Defence*, p. 142.

phical basis. Hooker is indeed one of the most important, though not the only, link between medieval and modern political philosophy in England. He provides the formal continuity of doctrines and ideas which were to become formidable weapons in the hands of later writers and controversialists; a formal continuity which is of course no excuse for overlooking the deep change which their meaning underwent in the completely secularized political theory of modern times. The influence of Hooker's teaching upon later generations is a fascinating subject of research. Hammond, Sanderson and Andrewes, Hales and Stillingfleet, Locke and Hoadly, Warburton and Tucker, Keble, Coleridge and Gladstone, make a list which is far from being complete. That such widely different thinkers and such eminent representatives of English thought have professed their admiration for Hooker as the result of a deep study of his work, is a proof that his lesson was not taught in vain and that his ideas and doctrines have become a lasting inheritance of the English mind.

VI

RICHARD HOOKER

I HAVE tried to explain Hooker's attitude towards the idea of the law of nature, and the reasons which account for the fact that, as Dean Church remarked, the outlines of Hooker's theory of law and politics 'are to be found in the great work of Thomas Aquinas'.

It is important, however, that we should ask ourselves whether this acceptance or restoration of traditional ideas was not accompanied by substantial qualifications, and whether the subtle changes which they underwent is not even more interesting than the formal continuity to which they seem to bear witness. I propose, in this concluding lecture, to illustrate some of these changes, or rather to recall the main points where the formal continuity of certain principles is no excuse for overlooking their substantial transformation in the further development of political thought.

The first point to which I should like to draw your attention is the value and meaning of the very idea of natural law. It has been pointed out many times that the doctrine of natural law played a prominent part in that secularization of politics which modern thought has achieved. Though certainly not the only element in that process, the idea of natural law thus appears, notwithstanding its formal continuity, as a determining factor in that break between medieval and modern political theory which is a crucial issue for the historian. The new school of natural law differed from the old one in several ways. It developed the conception of a thoroughly secular natural law, emancipated both from Scripture and tradition, and based

on reason alone, without any qualification; 'the product'—
as Professor Barker puts it—'of the free lucubration of
the legal philosopher, researching *in scrinio pectoris sui*'. It
is clearly in the light of such a development that Hooker's
theory of law must be viewed, if we are adequately to value
and interpret its meaning.

It is from the very definition of law that Hooker takes
up his position. His definition of law echoes almost word
for word the definition of Thomas Aquinas. Will and
command are not to him the constituent elements of law.
There is a close connexion between law and reason: law
is, as Aquinas had said, *aliquid rationis*. This idea has
far-reaching theological and philosophical implications.
Through the definition of law, the idea of reason is introduced into the very concept of God's nature; and it is the
principle of reason which in turn helps to bridge the gulf
between man's limitation and God's infinity. We are thus
led to an essentially hierarchical conception of the world:
for the dictates and working of reason vary according to the
scale of nature and the forms and ranks of creation, which
make up that 'admirable order, wherein God hath disposed
all laws, each as in nature, so in degree, distinct from
other'.[1] From the pure passivity of inanimate things, as
we 'lift up our eyes from the footstool to the throne of
God', we reach up to the consciousness of rational beings,
where the ultimate identification of law with reason is
made evident to man; for the law of human nature is the
law of reason, and reason is the means by which men
'learn in many things what the will of God is'.[2] This is
entirely in the line of the Thomist conception of the fundamental harmony of the natural and the supernatural, of a

[1] *Eccl. Pol.* I. xvi. 7.
[2] *Ibid.* I. viii. 3.

succession of degrees which lead in their progression from nature to God. How far it is remote from what is usually conceived to be the typical Protestant attitude towards these problems, may here be left out of discussion. The question is, rather, in what sense can Hooker be termed a rationalist on account of the stress which he lays on the powers and dignity of human nature. Does not the idea that the law of nature is deducible by man's reason alone imply that this law has a value and a meaning apart from any other consideration, apart even from God Himself— *licet Deus non esset?* Such a daring assertion had already been made by some of the Schoolmen, though not by Thomas himself;[1] and Grotius was soon to make it the corner-stone of a purely rational system of ethics. The idea that individual reason is a sufficient standard of action might thus seem to pave the way to the entirely secular and individualistic political theory of the seventeenth and eighteenth centuries.

It is clear, however, that any such implication is not only entirely lacking, but as it were neutralized by two important factors in Hooker's thought. The first is his acceptance of the scholastic and traditional idea of the law of nature as a part of the eternal order which God has imposed upon creation, and therefore as an objective scheme of divinely constituted realities and rules to which man has to adjust his life if he is to be true to his own divine essence. The other element, whose decisive influence is to be noticed, is Hooker's deep historical sense. No doubt the manner in which Hooker set himself to deduce the 'several grand mandates' of natural law, discoverable 'by discourse of natural reason', may seem to

---

[1] See the authors quoted in Suarez, *De Legibus,* II. xv; and Gierke, *Althusius,* p. 74.

suggest a rational deduction of morality, on the abstract lines of later thought. But when it comes to laying down the 'signs' by which the teaching of nature may be inferred, the grounds of conviction on which the mind needs to yield its assent, we find that what Hooker is enforcing is the value of historical certitude, the strong presumption in favour of that which has been traditionally held and accepted,[1] or carries with itself the approbation, not of the 'casual and unadvised sentences of men', but of 'the wisest and skilfullest part' of mankind. That this is a leading motive of Hooker's thought is well known to all readers of the *Laws of Ecclesiastical Polity*.

It is not, then, without important qualifications that Hooker may be termed a rationalist in his theory of natural law. His theory is divided from the rationalism of later days not only by the maintenance of the traditional theological background and the limits which he is careful to assign to the independence or autonomy of human reason, but also by his idea that rational constructions must stand the test of history and may not contradict the evidence of tradition and historical development. Some writers indeed have gone so far as to see in him a forerunner of the historical thinking of modern times, and to draw a parallel between him and Burke. But the fact that Hooker's teaching, from different angles, suggests different and opposite later developments, seems to me simply to prove how deeply his doctrines were rooted in the living development of the thought of his time. Moreover, as one of the greatest English exponents of the doctrine of natural law, Hooker gives us the clearest evidence of the subtle modifications which this doctrine underwent through the influence of the English mentality. The typically English distrust of

[1] *Eccl. Pol.* IV. iv. 2; v. I.

rational constructions and deep feeling for tradition, finds here its expression and stamps its characteristic mark on Hooker's doctrinal edifice.

It is in Hooker's treatment of human law that the outlines of his political theory begin to be apparent. The problem of human law was to him, as it had been to the Schoolmen, equivalent to that of political authority. He considered human laws, as did St. Thomas, as 'particular determinations' of the precept of the law of nature. They 'are made by politic societies: some, only as those societies are civilly united; some, as they are spiritually joined and make such a body as we call the church'.[1] The problem of the origin and nature both of state and church is thus opened. But before we proceed to examine what is perhaps the most discussed section of Hooker's political theory, I should like to call your attention to some very important issues, raised by Hooker's treatment of human law and closely related to the problems which have been under discussion in the preceding lectures.

Human laws are made necessary by the fact that men live 'joined with others in common society'.[2] They must take into account the stubbornness and depravity of man's mind and will, and be content to frame his outward actions in such a way as to direct them to a right end; they can do no more than this.[3] This is an important point: the object of human laws is and can only be outward action, they have no control over thoughts and feelings.[4] Hooker is thus led to throw light upon the vital difference between legal conformity and the moral value of action, and to emphasize the necessity of distinguishing between the two. 'Wherein appeareth also the difference between human and divine laws, the one of which two are

---

[1] *Ibid.* I. x. 11.   [2] *Ibid.* VIII. vi. 5.   [3] *Ibid.* I. x. 1; v. lxviii. 7.   [4] *Ibid.* I. xii. 2.

content with *opus operatum*, the other require *opus operantis*, the one do but claim the deed, the other especially the mind. So that according to laws which principally respect the heart of men, works of religion being not religiously performed, cannot be morally perfect.'[1] There is nothing particularly new, from a purely doctrinal standpoint, in such an assertion. That nothing but external acts can be the object of legal obligation had already been pointed out by Aquinas, and this does not logically imply a clear-cut division between the legal and the moral sphere, such as it was the work of modern philosophers, from Thomasius to Kant, firmly to establish. The real importance and interest of Hooker's handling of the question lies in my opinion in the inferences which he draws from his analysis of the formal and external character of positive human legislation. His theory has a striking affinity to that of Marsilius, and it is quite clear that Hooker was aware of the immediate bearing of the question upon the actual problems of Tudor religious policy. There is in fact an almost complete identity between Hooker's principles and the theory which underlies the official and unofficial defence of Elizabethan legislation. It is a theory which may imply at one and the same time a justification of political persecution, and an acknowledgement of religious liberty or toleration. 'As opinions do cleave to the understanding, and are in heart assented unto, it is not the power of any human law to command them, because to prescribe what men shall think belongeth only unto God.... As opinions are either fit or inconvenient to be professed, so man's law hath to determine of them.'[2] It is precisely on this same ground that those chiefly responsible for Elizabethan persecution took their stand when they proclaimed their

---

[1] *Eccl. Pol.* v. lxii. 15.   [2] *Ibid.* VIII. vi. 5.

respect for 'freedom of conscience', and asserted that the security of the State was the only object of the government's action: that, in other words, they were punishing not religious opinion, but political behaviour.[1] I cannot examine here the complete development of this theory;[2] but I have said enough in dealing with the same argument in Marsilius to show the sophism upon which it is grounded and which makes it so ludicrously inadequate as a defence. Undoubtedly Hooker's distinction contains the germ of a theory of toleration; but it is toleration of a very particular kind: toleration, which may amount to the acknowledgement of liberty of conscience within the bounds of the church, but not of religious liberty within the state. For, on the one hand, the enforcement of religious opinion is neither expedient nor possible and the best course for the church is to strive after conciliation and comprehension; while, on the other hand, outward conformity can and must be compulsory when this is necessary 'for public unity's sake'.[3] I need not remind you how deeply the very existence and fate of the Church of England were to be entangled in these issues in the following century.

We have seen that Hooker conceives of human positive law as a 'determination' of the law of nature. This implies a definite notion of its limits. Hooker's theory of the relation of human law to natural law is that of Aquinas, the

---

[1] This idea is already expressed in the *Declaration of the Queen's proceedings since her reign* of 1570, and is further developed in that official defence of Elizabeth's policy, *The Execution of Justice in England* of 1583, the work very likely of Burghley himself. Exactly the same line is taken by Bacon in his *Observations on a libel*, 1592 (*Works*, ed. Spedding, viii) and in a letter of Walsingham (1589/90) probably drafted by him (*ibid.*).

[2] See W. K. Jordan, *The development of religious toleration in England*, vol. i. (From the beginning of the English Reformation to the death of Queen Elizabeth.) London, 1932.

[3] *Eccl. Pol.* VIII. vi. 5.

traditional doctrine of the unconditional supremacy of a moral and religious code embodied in the law of nature and in the revealed law of God. But when it comes to the problem of a possible opposition or conflict between human law and the higher laws of nature and God, and of its consequences upon the bonds of obedience, Hooker's teaching is extremely guarded and shifting. Clearly, an abstract theory of resistance is not to be expected from a loyal Elizabethan divine, and it is important enough that the problem should have been discussed, as we shall see, in its more political aspect.

Within the limits of natural and divine law Hooker makes the strongest possible assertion of the full and complete power of the human legislator. Within these limits, societies, both civil and spiritual, may exercise their lawful and sovereign power. Those things which the law of God and of nature 'leaveth arbitrary and at liberty are all subject unto positive laws of men; which laws, for the common benefit, abridge particular men's liberty in such things as far as the rules of equity will suffer. This we must either maintain, or else overturn the world and make every man his own commander.'[1] We have seen that the point had an immediate controversial bearing; but it is important to notice that it is from this essentially traditional teaching that later theorists were to evolve that doctrine of the ἀδιάφορα which played such an important part in defining the proper sphere of political sovereignty.[2] It is upon this ground that, in meeting the *iure divino* claim of his Puritan opponents, Hooker develops that theory of the mutability of human laws which

[1] *Eccl. Pol.* v. lxxi. 5.

[2] See above, p. 110; the same position with regard to the 'things indifferent' is taken by Hutton (afterwards Archbishop of York) in a letter to Burghley of 1573 (quoted in Wordsworth, *Ecclesiastical Biography*, iii, 1853, note to p. 542–3).

is perhaps the aspect of his theory most deeply influenced by his feeling for history and where the realism with which he considered the problem of politics is most apparent. The laws of ecclesiastical—and *a fortiori* of civil—polity, are removed from the control of a rigid appeal to the Bible and conceived in terms of historical convenience and development. It is the aim of Hooker's system of laws to determine the comparative independence, with regard to the fundamental principles of Christianity, of human legislation, and to show that it is by its nature subject to change and capable of progressive transformation.

However important his abstract treatment of the nature and character of laws may be for a correct interpretation of Hooker's thought, it is not this which usually attracts attention, but rather his theory of the origins and grounds of political authority. The frequent misconstructions of Hooker's teaching in this respect have led to much confusion, and this reaches its height in the question of his acceptance of the doctrine of the social contract and of popular sovereignty. That Hooker's theory of politics is founded upon a contractual premiss is a view which has not been without authoritative supporters even in quite recent times: nor is there anything new in its refutation. But perhaps the best-known attempt to read back a theory of contract into Hooker's political theory is that for which Locke is responsible. The interest of Locke's tendentious reading of Hooker lies not only in a comparison between Hooker's conception and that of one of the most extreme and complete exponents of the idea of social contract, but in the particular value which Locke attributed to Hooker as a forerunner of this doctrine, thus endeavouring to present his own theory as a vindication of the old and traditional doctrine concerning the origin and foundation of political society. A survey of the several quotations from Hooker in the second *Treatise of Civil Government* provides the best evidence of the possibility of such an interpretation; and it is important to notice that Locke's quotations are, on the whole, verbally correct, and that all of them are drawn from the first book of the *Ecclesiastical Polity*, the genuineness of which could never be questioned.

The natural and original freedom and equality of men, which is the foundation of the contractual theory, was to Locke an axiom of natural law, openly acknowledged by the 'judicious' Hooker. An immediate consequence of that principle is the idea of the state of nature: 'to those that say there were never any men in the state of nature', Locke opposed the authority of Hooker. Hooker was perfectly clear that it is possible to think of mankind as living independently of any form of political organization, but he asserted the 'natural inclination' of man towards social life, and Locke agreed with him. To put an end to the inconveniences of such a condition, men have come to agreement among themselves and have established political authority. Whatever may have been its historical origins —and both Locke and Hooker admit of a progressive growth from paternal government—every government, every state, 'all public regiment', goes back ultimately to some formal expression of human will, to 'deliberate advice, consultation and composition between men' (*Eccl. Pol.* i, x, 4). 'Common consent' is therefore the foundation and justification of civil power, since no man may presume nor claim any power over other men without their consent. The conclusion from these premisses is clearly drawn by Hooker, and emphatically repeated by Locke: the community is the origin and source of political power, except in the case of a direct intervention or designation on the part of God. Finally, having supported with Hooker's authority his theory of the origin and foundations of political power, Locke tried to show that his theory of the ends and limits of this power derived from the same source. The common good is the end of political organization. Its limits are set by the law of nature, which goes back ultimately to the will of God and appears as the measure of positive law and the condition of its validity. Positive law, which admits of no exception towards any member of the community, is the guarantee of political organization against all arbitrary action of the individual. The power of establishing that law belongs originally and fundamentally to the whole community.

I have thought it useful to make this brief summary of the clear and coherent doctrine which Locke succeeded in reading into Hooker's text, because it represents the best illustration of the possibility of interpreting Hooker's teaching as a striking anticipation of the modern doctrine of social contract and popular sovereignty. A careful examination of the very substantial differences which separate these later developments from Hooker's position is the only way to secure a just estimate of his views on this question. The widely different implications and meaning of the apparently identical conceptions upon which Hooker's and Locke's political theories are based, follow as a consequence of the radical divergence of the philosophical standpoints of their authors. I have already given some hint of this in talking of the difference between the traditional and the new theory of natural law. Let us take, for instance, Hooker's assertion of the 'natural' freedom and equality of men. This was to Hooker not only a moral and religious principle, but also one of whose political implications he was fully conscious. It implies, in fact, a refusal to accept the Aristotelian doctrine of the natural inequality of men as an adequate explanation and justification of political power. But this refusal implies no assertion of 'natural rights' in the individual, prior to and independent of the state. It simply recognizes the 'conventional' character of political organization, as revealed in the contrast between the actual conditions of organized life, and an original condition, corresponding to the 'state of nature', of which the notion, if not the expression, is clearly to be found in Hooker. Hooker admits, it is true, a 'natural inclination' in man towards 'sociable life and fellowship'; but it is quite clear that political organization may only claim a secondary, not a primary value, and is not 'natural', in the Aristotelian sense, as being a condition of human perfection. It is, in fact, a consequence of human corruption, the divinely appointed remedy for the evil tendencies of human nature. All this is quite obviously in the line of traditional Christian political theory. As Dr. Carlyle has rightly pointed out, there is here a proof that this traditional doctrine was so firmly rooted, that not even St. Thomas's great authority succeeded in shaking it, and that the revival of the Aristotelian doctrine left very little trace in the development of political theory.

The fact that political authority is made necessary by the actual 'corruption of our nature' does not, however, according to Hooker, exclude the human will from being called to play a prominent part in its creation and establishment. But to acknowledge that political organization is in some way dependent upon the will of its components is something very different from conceiving of it in the rigid terms of a contract. Let me recall, to simplify the discussion in this respect, the distinction, which is familiar to the student of political theory, between the two main forms which the contractual idea has assumed in the development of political thought: the distinction between the agreement among all to unite, the *pactum unionis* or *societatis*, and the agreement with a sovereign to obey, the *pactum subiectionis*. It is needless to add that it is not always easy to draw this distinction in the complex development of contractual theory, where the two notions appear very often closely mingled together. There can, however, be little doubt that the contract which becomes in the seventeenth and eighteenth centuries the commonly accepted starting-point of political speculation and finds its complete development in Locke's political theory, is a contract between individuals, that is, the social contract proper, or *pactum societatis*. The importance of Hooker's theory and its apparent analogy with Locke's theory of the social contract may seem to consist in his assertion of an agreement between individuals, which is the characteristic element of the *pactum societatis*. Hooker, indeed, seems to conceive of men as co-operating deliberately to the establishment of political authority. It is this deliberate act of union by individuals which, according to Mr. Gough and to several interpreters before him, is the stamp of a social contract. But here again it is necessary to submit Hooker's words to very careful examination. This recognition of the voluntary origin of political organization is a consequence of the rejection, which we have just examined, of the Aristotelian conception of the 'natural' foundation of the state. The idea of the *pactum societatis*, on the other hand, derives its vital importance in the history of political philosophy from its appearance as the coherent development of the principle of the natural rights of individual personality. It may well be doubted, I think, whether Hooker's words contain any assertion of that 'individualist principle' which Mr. Gough has thought it possible to see in them. It is doubtful indeed whether they may fairly be said to contain at all the idea of a contract. The very notion of contract as a manifestation of will, with the object of establishing a relationship of mutual obligation, is entirely lacking. The agreement between men which Hooker describes, appears on a closer examination as little more than the common purpose of accepting 'some kind of government public, and [of] yielding themselves subject thereunto'.[1] It is, at any rate, clear enough that there is no place in Hooker's conception for that implicit opposition between the individual and the state, and for that mechanical construction of society, which characterizes the doctrine of the social contract in its later developments. On the contrary, as we shall presently see, the very backbone of Hooker's political conception is the idea of the community as a living organism and an historical growth.

Although, however, the constituent element of the 'state' cannot be said to lie for Hooker in a *pactum societatis* or social contract proper, we do find some traces in his political theory of the idea of a contract viewed as a *pactum subiectionis*. This is in fact the form in which the idea usually appears in sixteenth-century political theory. The foundation of that conception, the principle, that is, that political power derives from the community as its original source, is clearly and explicitly set down by Hooker. It is, however, subject to the important and traditional qualification of the divine foundation and sanction of all legitimate authority. But the vindication of the original power of the whole society remains undoubtedly one of the distinctive marks of Hooker's poli-

[1] *Eccl. Pol.* I. x. 4.

tical theory, and it is important to notice that the principle is found clearly stated in the first book, before being fully developed in the eighth. It may indeed be this development in the eighth book, as Mr. Houk has recently suggested, which accounts for its delayed publication, as it certainly does for the doubts which were later to be thrown upon its authenticity. I am sorry not to be able to enter into a detailed examination of these developments, as well as of the brief but open mention of the *pactum subiectionis* which can be found in the eighth book. The relationship between the king and the people as the original source of power is there discussed in detail, and the problem of resistance is actually raised upon contractual premisses. But it is important to note that far from developing the principle thus laid down into an abstract construction of the state on democratic premisses, Hooker endeavoured to ground it in experience and history. He conceived of it as a constitutional principle, which he applied and made use of in his discussion of the best form of government and of the actual problems of the English constitution.

One last doubt may arise in connexion with the question which we have so far discussed. It regards the proper meaning of the principle, which Hooker vigorously asserts, that consent is the only justification of power. In such an assertion, however, there is no ground for inferring a recognition or a vindication of original or 'natural' rights in the individual or in society. The principle is quite consistent with the traditional medieval doctrine of consent as the foundation of political authority, which has been sketched in the preceding lectures. It is clear that in itself the principle entirely lacks that subjectivism which later political theorists, like Locke, attached to it. They

conceived of it as the necessary consequence of the
'natural' freedom and equality, the fundamental 'natural
rights', of the individual. But far from indulging in such
an abstract interpretation, Hooker here again always kept
constitutional facts and historical experience in mind.
This appears in his efforts to produce evidence of the
several ways in which consent may, directly or indirectly,
by means of representation or custom, and always with
regard to the organic and not individualistic structure of
society, be manifested or presupposed as the foundation
of established authority.

Next in importance to the question of the origins and
foundations of society, the problem of the power which
is to hold society together is one of the crucial points of
Hooker's discussion of the problem of politics. Whether
Hooker attained a clear grasp of the idea of sovereignty
or gave a coherent solution to its momentous problems is
an interesting problem. There is a very important remark
on this point by his friend George Cranmer, to whom he
had submitted his manuscript for criticism. 'I could
wishe,' wrote the latter in one of his notes on the sixth
book,[1] 'that in this discourse and in the whole body of your
booke wheresoever mention is made of τὸ κύριον, you should
give yt the same name. You terme yt sometymes chiefety
of dominion, sometymes souverainety, sometymes im-
periall power. . . .' This is no doubt a proof of a certain
uneasiness on Hooker's part about the use of a word and
notion which Bodin's celebrated work had just brought
into circulation, in England as over all Europe. But

---

[1] These notes were printed by Keble in an appendix to Book VI, from the
manuscript preserved in Corpus library. It appears from the fact that they
almost entirely disagree with the presently received text of this book, that the
original text must have been a very different work, and may have contained
important remarks upon the problems with which we are here concerned.

another reason for doubting whether a clear notion of sovereignty can be looked for in Hooker is his deliberate refusal to construct his theory of law upon a purely voluntaristic basis, which, as we have seen, is a distinctive feature of his whole system of ethics. Nevertheless, as I have tried to show, one of the recurring motives of Hooker's theory of human law is his assertion of the full and complete power of the human legislator within the limits of natural and divine law. Thus—although within the frame of an intellectualistic conception of law—the problem of sovereignty could not be avoided: nor could it possibly be otherwise in such a controversy as that with the Puritans, which involved, as we know, the whole problem of allegiance.

'The public power of all societies is above every soul contained in the same societies.'[1] This supremacy is the very condition of the existence of society. It consists, for Hooker as for Bodin, in the power of making laws, and belongs to 'politic societies', that is, to the 'several bodies politic', or 'nations' which constitute the units of political life. There is no higher authority above that of the single body politic, except the very vague and general one of a super or international law which Hooker calls the 'law of nations', the notion of which is, however, neither fully nor clearly developed. The problem, which raises the more interesting issues in Hooker's political theory, is that of the actual distribution of power within the body politic as the sovereign unit and the ultimate source of authority. For this entailed a careful discussion of the problem of the English constitution and law in relation to the notion of sovereignty. As if aware of the difficulties in which a coherent development of the doctrine of the derivation of power from the community would involve

[1] *Eccl. Pol.* I. xvi. 5.

him, Hooker deliberately restricted the field of his inquiry to his own country: 'That we be not enforced to make over-large discourse about the different conditions of sovereign or supreme power, that which we speak of kings shall be with respect to the state and according to the nature of this kingdom.'[1] It has seemed that this apparent limitation to particular historical conditions is one sign of the inferiority of Hooker's thought, and that of political thought in England generally in the sixteenth century, in comparison with contemporary continental thought. Both Professor Holdsworth and Mr. Gooch have taken the view that Elizabethan political theory is interesting for the insight which it provides into Tudor public opinion, but that it is insular, and entirely lacks the great conflict of principles and ideas which give lasting value to political speculation. Such a judgement seems to me unfair to Hooker. The great problems of contemporary political thought were present to him even in his discussion of questions peculiar to England. In his attempt, for instance, to uphold the traditional view of the derivation of power from the community, or, as he calls it, of 'the King's dependency' on the 'whole entire body, over the several parts whereof he hath dominion', without accepting the 'strange, untrue, and unnatural conceits, set abroad by seedsmen of rebellion', he is directly condemning the doctrine of the *Vindiciae contra Tyrannos*, and in fact of the whole left wing of sixteenth-century political theory.[2] In his defence of a constitutionally limited monarchy, such as he conceived the English to be, he appears to be clearly aware of the issues involved in the position which he defends.[3] Although he does not here refer to Bodin, it is tempting to consider the whole discussion as an answer

[1] *Eccl. Pol.* VIII. ii. 7.   [2] *Ibid.* VIII. ii. 8.   [3] *Ibid.* VIII. ii. 11–13.

to the difficulties which Bodin (with whose work Hooker was certainly acquainted) had raised with regard to the constitution of England in the name of his sharply drawn conception of sovereignty.[1] But the chief interest of Hooker's praise of the English constitution lies in the manner in which he contrived to adapt traditional conceptions, which he himself traces as far back as Bracton, to the new and modern requirements of a country which had undergone since the close of the Middle Ages a thorough transformation. The old ideas of consent, of the supremacy of law, of a mixed constitution, of representation, all converge in Hooker's conception, and afford a striking illustration of the manner in which medieval doctrines could be developed to meet the necessities of political development.

There still remains to be examined an idea which often recurs in Hooker, and whose correct appreciation is necessary to an understanding both of those problems which have already been discussed, and of that—the problem of religious organization—which still remains to be dealt with. I would call it the idea of the unity of the political body, but it may also be called by a modern name, the idea of the sovereignty and personality of the state. Professor Holdsworth has remarked that no lawyer nor statesman of the Tudor period

'could have given an answer to the question or to the wherewithal

---

[1] Jean Bodin, *De la République*, livre I, ch. 8 (ed. 1593, pp. 139 ff.). It is interesting to compare Bodin's judgement of the English constitution with that given, at about the same time, by the Italian writer Botero (*Relazioni Universali*, 1591–96, p. II, l. i). Curiously enough, a vivid refutation of the theory of limited monarchy in the name of the principle of sovereignty is to be found in the work of Hooker's friend Hadrian Saravia, *De Imperandi Authoritate et Christiana Obedientia*, London, 1593. Mr. Houk has recently thrown some doubts upon Walton's account of the intimate friendship between Hooker and Saravia.

of the sovereign power in the English state. The doctrine of sovereignty was a new doctrine in the sixteenth century; nor is it readily grasped until the existence of a conflict between several competitors for political power makes it necessary to decide which of these various competitors can in the last resort enforce its will. . . . Till then general assertions as to the supremacy of some particular person or body of persons will serve.'

Elizabethan writers like Sir Thomas Smith or Hooker contented themselves with such a general assertion of the supremacy of the king in Parliament, but the assertion is important enough; for it implies nothing less than the assertion of the unity of the English nation and of its absolute sovereignty.

'The parliament of England together with the convocation annexed thereunto, is that whereupon the very essence of all government within this kingdom doth depend; it is even the body of the whole realm; it consisteth of the king, and of all that within the land are subject unto him: for they all are there present, either in person or by such as they voluntarily have derived their very personal right unto.'[1]

It is this conception of the political body as a unit and a living organism which gives to Hooker's, and to the legal and political theory of the Tudor period, a capital importance; for as Maitland has pointed out, a conception is foreshadowed in it which was only to be fully grasped by political theorists of much later days, the conception of the personality and sovereignty of the state. It is in this conception that, at the close of the century, Hooker sums up, as it were, the lesson of the Tudor experiment. It is this conception which we must bear in mind in order to understand Hooker's treatment of the problem which provides the title of his work, the problem of the '*Laws of Ecclesiastical Polity*'. 'Laws human are made by politic

[1] *Eccl. Pol.* VIII. vi. 11.

societies: some, only as those societies are civilly united; some as they are spiritually joined and make such a body as we call the church.'[1] A conception of the church is here implied which Hooker never contradicts in his different attempts to define more closely the essentials of religious organization. In a further analysis he distinguishes indeed between the church as a natural and as a supernatural society,[2] between the mystical and the visible body of the church.[3] But the visible church, sharing the character of a 'politic society', reproduces the features of political organization:

'As the main body of the sea being one, yet within divers precincts hath divers names; so the Catholic Church is in like sort divided into a number of distinct societies, every one of which is termed a Church within itself . . . unto every of which the name of a Church is given with addition betokening severalty, as the Church of Rome, Corinth, Ephesus, England, and so the rest.'[4]

What, then, is the difference between one particular church and one particular state, between, say, the church and the commonwealth of England? If a church is nothing else than a 'politic society' under its religious aspect, clearly, there can be no such difference and, provided that the state is Christian, the state is itself a church. To prove that in a Christian community church and state cannot be conceived as distinct and opposed societies but as coincident, is the main theme of the first chapters of the eighth book of Hooker's *Ecclesiastical Polity*. It is the doctrine which Archbishop Whitgift had taught in plain and open words, the doctrine in which Canterbury agreed with Zürich against Geneva and Rome: 'I make no difference betwixt a Christian commonwealth and the Church

---

[1] *Eccl. Pol.* I. x. 11.   [2] *Ibid.* I. xv.   [3] *Ibid.* III. i.
[4] *Ibid.* III. i. 14.

of Christ'—'urbem Christianam nihil quam Ecclesiam Christianam esse'.[1]

We are thus brought back once again to the question of the practical organization of the Christian ideal. You may perhaps have noticed that it is in his estimate of the Anglican theory in the light of the ideal of the *respublica christiana* that Figgis is at his best. But it is difficult to say what exactly is the outcome of his brilliant generalizations. For on one side it would appear that he considers the indignant rejection by such writers as Whitgift and Hooker, of the notion that church and state are two distinct societies, as a proof of the traditional character of the idea of *respublica christiana*. Yet on the other hand Figgis himself has given instances of the novelty of the official Anglican doctrine by recalling the contempt and hatred with which it was regarded by Puritan and Jesuit alike as 'Machiavellistica et Turcica'. Here again a clear notion of the issues of medieval political thought may be of some help in forming an adequate estimate of the traditional elements and of the actual novelty in Hooker's position.

'We hold, that seeing there is not any man of the Church of England but the same man is also a member of the commonwealth; nor any man a member of the commonwealth, which is not also of the Church of England; therefore as in a figure triangular the base doth differ from the sides thereof, and yet one and the selfsame line is both a base and also a side; a side simply, a base if it chance to be the bottom and underlie the rest: so, albeit properties and actions of one kind do cause the name of a commonwealth, qualities and functions of another sort the name of a Church to be given unto a multitude,

---

[1] Whitgift, *Works*, iii, p. 313; Zwingli, *Opera*, ed. Schuler and Schulthess, VI, 1, 6, quot. by Farner, *Die Lehre von Kirche und Staat bei Zwingli*, 1930, p. 132. For the correspondence between the Anglican and the Zwinglian teaching see above, p. 104, note 1, and Maitland, in *Cambridge Mod. History*, ii, pp. 597–8.

yet one and the selfsame multitude may in such sort be both, and is so with us, that no person appertaining to the one can be denied to be also of the other.'[1]

It is in this famous comparison that Hooker illustrates his conception of the coincidence of state and church in the Christian community. The very condition of this coincidence is such as to distinguish Hooker's teaching from the Erastian theory of later days: the condition, namely, that this coincidence can only happen where the state accepts true religion and is based upon religious uniformity. Hence it follows that if the state is unchristian, or in a society in which there is no such uniformity, the church must be conceived as an autonomous and independent body; but it follows also and primarily that, within the Christian state, there is no place for divided allegiance, and indeed the bond of religious is identical with that of political obligation. Hooker is perfectly clear on the subject. 'Our question is one of dominion' he declares, and he goes on to show how division will cause 'inevitable destruction':

'Wherefore . . . there must of necessity in all public societies be a general mover, directing unto the common good, and framing every man's particular to it. . . . Such as in one public state have agreed that the supreme charge of all things should be committed unto one, they, I say, were for fear of those inconveniences withdrawn from liking to establish many, . . . Surely two supreme masters would make any one man's service somewhat uneasy in such cases as might fall out. Suppose that to-morrow the power which hath dominion in justice require thee at the court; that which in war, at the field; that which in religion, at the temple: all have equal authority over thee, and impossible it is, that thou shouldest be in such case obedient to all: by choosing any one whom thou wilt obey, certain thou art for thy disobedience to incur the displeasure of the other two.'[2]

---

[1] *Eccl. Pol.* VIII. i. 2.   [2] *Ibid.* VIII. ii. 18.

Hooker is clearly here reaping the fruit of an historical as well as doctrinal development which goes back to the very beginning of the Reformation in this country. The principle of unity which he lays down is exactly the same as that which had been proclaimed in the *Statute of Appeals*, and the implications of which had been clearly grasped by contemporaries. The argument against divided allegiance is the central one in the Anglican position from Gardiner to Hooker, and is repeated almost word for word by both at a distance of over half a century.[1] It is an argument which could hold good against old Priest as well as against new Presbyter, as Whitgift, Bancroft, and Sutcliffe had quickly detected.[2] The rejection of any *imperium in imperio*, the denial of the right to existence of any organization whatsoever, parallel or rival to the state is, as was pointed out by later and more liberal-minded Churchmen, such as Bishop Warburton, a striking anticipation of Hobbes.[3] But it is also a direct reminiscence of Marsilius, and Professor Previté-Orton has traced the parallel in detail.

[1] Gardiner, *On true obedience*, ed. Heywood, pp. 54–6: 'Seeing the Church of England consisteth of the same sorts of people at this day that are comprised in this word, Realm, of whom the King is called the Head: shall he not, being called the Head of the Realm of England, be also the Head of the same men when they are named the Church of England? If the King be the Head of the Realm, that is as much as a man would say, he hath so many as are within the dominion of the Realm, united all unto himself as unto one body, that they may take him for their supreme head, can it be by any possible means through the mutation of the name, for all one selfsame man, to be in subjection to this head, and not to be in subjection to this head in all one kind of subjection, that is to say, for God's sake? For there is no subjection against God.—What a folly were it then for a man to confess, that all one man (if ye lust to call him Johan) dwelling in England, is in subjection to the King, as unto the head; and if ye call him a Christian, of the same sorte, to say that he is not a subject?'

[2] Whitgift, *Works*, iii, p. 295–306; Bancroft, *Sermon preached at Paules Crosse*, p. 71; Matthew Sutcliffe, *A Treatise of Ecclesiasticall Discipline*, London, 1591, p. 147.

[3] *The Alliance between Church and State*, book II, ch. v, in *Works*, ed. 1788, pp. 185–6.

And yet, when all this is said, let us not be misled by this high and resounding vindication of the sovereignty and unity of the state. For there is an element in Hooker's position which is very far indeed both from Marsilius and from Hobbes, and which accounts for the fact that he remains in the line of Christian thought rather than in that of state-worship past or present. This element is his refusal to admit that the Christian ideal may yield to political necessities. The first chapters of the fifth book contain an emphatic condemnation of Machiavelli and of 'the politic use of religion', together with a moving vindication of the dependence of politics on the higher standards of religion and ethics. It is difficult to understand, when we read these pages, how recent German interpreters have ventured to speak, in reference to Hooker's idealization of English church-policy, of a suspicious coincidence between 'reason of state' and 'ecclesiastical wisdom'.[1] That the Elizabethan settlement not only proved most favourable to the 'interest of the state', but was actually devised by unscrupulous politicians to square with the needs of a ruthless policy of national autonomy can of course hardly be denied. But it is to say the least grossly unfair to suppose that a pious and deeply religious mind such as Hooker's might have envisaged the problem of the church from the new angle of 'reason of state', or, even worse, have accepted some of its newly discovered axioms as an adequate defence and justification of his beloved *Ecclesia Anglicana*. He is thoroughly medieval—or shall we say more generally Christian?—in conceiving of the duties and task of the Christian state towards true religion. True

[1] P. Schütz, *Religion und Politik in der Kirche von England*, Gotha, 1925 ; W. Pauck, *Das Reich Gottes auf Erden*. Eine Untersuchung . . . zur englischen Staatskirche des 16ten Jahrhunderts, Berlin, 1928 ; H. Leube, *Reformation und Humanismus in England*, Leipzig, 1930.

religion appears as the goal to which the state must tend, and this is at bottom entirely independent of the competence and power of the state itself. Hooker is on this point as far as Erastus from the Erastianism of the following century. He draws indeed the lesson from a particular national venture, but he also succeeds in raising this lesson to the dignity of a principle: the principle that there need be no anxiety as to the condition of religion so long as the national conscience keeps faith with the main dictates of Christianity. How deeply this conciliation between national consciousness and the Christian ideal, to which Hooker's work bears witness, has gone to the root of much that is English, you are no doubt in a better condition to judge than I am. That it has left deep traces upon English political life cannot be better proved than by the words of a great English and Christian statesman, Gladstone, who summarized Hooker's position as expressing 'the great doctrine that the State is a person, having a conscience, cognisant of matter of religion, and bound by all constitutional and natural means to advance it'.[1] This idea of the dependence of state-power and state-action on higher and indeed eternal values is not so much a legacy of medieval as of Christian political thought. To reject it can only mean to renounce Christianity altogether, and to raise the state or the tribe to the place which the Christian reserves for God alone.

[1] *The State in its relation with the Church*, London, 1841, vol. i, p. 14.

A NOTE ABOUT THE LITERATURE

THE following list contains only outstanding and easily accessible works and a few other items to which the author desires to call attention. It is designed for the use of English readers.

First comes a list of books which deal with the whole subject or possess a general interest:

OTTO GIERKE, *Political Theories of the Middle Ages,* trans. F. W. Maitland, Cambridge, 1900, reprinted 1913, 1922. [This is a section in a chapter of Gierke's great work, *Das deutsche Genossenschaftsrecht,* 3 vols., 1868–81. Another important section, *Natural Law and the Theory of Society,* trans. E. Barker, vol. i, Cambridge, 1934, should also be noted. The introductions by Maitland and Barker are important.]

R. W. and A. J. CARLYLE, *A History of Medieval Political Theory in the West,* 6 vols., Edinburgh, 1903–36. [A standard work.]

C. H. MCILWAIN, *The Growth of Political Thought in the West from the Greeks to the end of the Middle Ages,* London, 1932.

ERNST TROELTSCH, *Die Soziallehren der christlichen Kirchen und Gruppen,* 3rd ed., Tübingen, 1923; trans. O. Wyon, *The Social Teaching of the Christian Churches,* 2 vols., New York, 1931. [This is a rather more difficult book, especially useful for the Christian premises of medieval political thought. Troeltsch's essay on 'The Ideas of Natural Law and Humanity', translated by Professor Barker and added to his translation of Gierke (see above), might be read first.]

J. W. GOUGH, *The Social Contract: a Critical Study of its Development,* Oxford, 1936.

PHYLLIS DOYLE, *A History of Political Thought,* 2nd ed., London, 1937. [A short analysis.] See also E. F. Jacob on political thought in *The Legacy of the Middle Ages,* 2nd ed., Oxford, 1932; W. H. V. Reade on political thought to *c.* 1300, in *The Cambridge Medieval History,* vol. vi, Cambridge, 1929; and H. J. Laski on political theory in the later Middle Ages, in the same, vol. viii, 1936.

Two German books which are especially helpful:

E. BERNHEIM, *Mittelalterliche Zeitanschauungen in ihrem Einfluss auf Politik und Geschichtsschreibung,* Tübingen, 1918.

F. KERN, *Gottesgnadentum und Widerstandsrecht im früheren Mittelalter,* Leipzig, 1915. [A well-known essay by J. N. Figgis, *The Divine Right of Kings,* 2nd ed., Cambridge, 1922, deals with the same subject.]

Lecture I

In addition to the books already mentioned:

R. L. Poole, *Illustrations of Medieval Thought*, London, 1884; 2nd and revised ed., 1920. [A famous work.]

E. Gilson, *The Spirit of Medieval Philosophy*, London, 1936.

J. N. Figgis, 'Respublica Christiana', an essay in *Churches in the Modern State*, 2nd ed., London, 1914; and the same writer's *Political Aspects of St. Augustine's 'City of God'*, London, 1921.

H. X. Arquillière, *L'Augustinisme politique; essai sur la formation des théories politiques du moyen âge*, Paris, 1934.

P. Vinogradoff, *Roman Law in Medieval Europe*, 2nd ed., Oxford, 1929. [Revised by F. de Zulueta; see also Vinogradoff on customary law and E. Meynial on Roman law in *The Legacy of the Middle Ages*.]

F. M. Powicke, 'Reflections on the Medieval State', in *Transactions of the Royal Hist. Society*, 4th series, vol. xix, 1936.

E. Lewis, 'Organic Tendencies in Medieval Political Thought' in *The American Political Science Review*, vol. xxxii, no. 5 (October 1938). [This remarkable article, which appeared when these lectures were in print, may be consulted for the points discussed on pp. 27–9 and for the whole question of medieval and Christian 'individualism'.]

Lecture II. *Thomas Aquinas*

The more important sections of the *Summa Theologica* relating to social and political problems have recently been published, together with a French translation, by the 'Revue des Jeunes', in small and handy volumes:

La Loi, Paris, 1935 (*Summa Theol.*, 1ª2ae, qu. 90–7).

La Justice, 3 vols., Paris, 1932–5 (*Summa Theol.*, 2ª2ae, qu. 57–79).

Les Vertus Sociales, Paris, 1931 (*Summa Theol.*, 2ª2ae, qu. 101–22).

The *Summa contra Gentiles* has been translated by the English Dominican Fathers, London, 1923 ff. (Read especially Book III, chapters 114–18, 128–30.) The most convenient edition of the *De regimine principum* is that of Mathis, Turin, 1924.

For St. Thomas and his thought, with some indication of the vast literature, see:

M. Grabmann, *Thomas Aquinas, his Personality and Thought*, New York, 1928.

E. Gilson, *The Philosophy of St. Thomas Aquinas*, Cambridge, 1929.

M. C. D'Arcy, *Thomas Aquinas*, London, 1930.

A. G. Sertillanges, *St. Thomas Aquinas and his Work*, London, 1932.

Also the books by R. W. and A. J. Carlyle, and by McIlwain noted above.

Three helpful books on the movement of thought at this time and at that of Marsilius, are:

C. N. S. Woolf, *Bartolus of Sassoferrato*, Cambridge, 1913.

J. Rivière, *Le problème de l'Église et de l'État au temps de Philippe le Bel*, Louvain, 1926.

G. de Lagarde, *Le naissance de l'esprit laïque au déclin du moyen âge*, vol. i, St. Paul-Trois-Châteaux, 1934.

Lectures III and IV. *Marsilius*

There are two admirable editions of the *Defensor Pacis*:

The Defensor Pacis of Marsilius of Padua, ed. C. W. Previté-Orton, Cambridge, 1928.

Marsilius von Padua, Defensor Pacis, ed. R. Scholz, Hanover, 1932–3. (Fontes juris germanici antiqui.)

On his life and thought see:

C. K. Brampton's paper on the life, and C. W. Previté-Orton's paper on the thought, in the *English Historical Review*, vols. xxxvii (1922) and xxxviii (1923); also, and still better, Professor Previté-Orton's lecture in the *Proceedings of the British Academy*, vol. xxi (1935).

The second volume of G. de Lagarde's *La naissance de l'esprit laïque*, mentioned above, deals with Marsilius. One of the latest essays on Marsilius, by his editor, R. Scholz, is in the *Historische Zeitschrift*, vol. clvi (1936).

The most notable discussions in the more general books already noted will be found in Poole's *Illustrations of Medieval Thought* and McIlwain's *Growth of Political Thought*.

Lectures V and VI. *Hooker*

The standard edition of the *Ecclesiastical Polity* is in Hooker's complete Works, with Isaac Walton's *Life of Hooker*, arranged by John Keble, 7th ed., revised by R. W. Church and Francis Paget, 3 vols., Oxford, 1888. A convenient edition is included in the 'Everyman Library', 2 vols., London [1907], with an introduction by R. Bayne. A scholarly edition of the eighth book, with a critical discussion of the question of its authenticity, was published by R. A. Houk, Columbia University Press, 1931.

For Hooker and his significance see:

J. W. Allen, *A History of Political Thought in the Sixteenth Century*, London, 1928.

A. P. d'Entrèves, *Riccardo Hooker. Contributo alla teoria e alla storia del diritto naturale*, Turin, 1932.

F. Paget, *Introduction to Book V of the Ecclesiastical Polity*, 2nd ed., Oxford, 1908.

It is essential, in reading Hooker, to understand the problems of his age.

The following books and articles should especially be noted:

Otto Gierke, *Johannes Althusius und die Entwicklung der naturrechtlichen Staatstheorien*, 4th ed., Breslau, 1929.

F. W. Maitland, *English Law and the Renaissance*, Cambridge, 1901; also his chapter on the Anglican settlement in the *Cambridge Modern History*, vol. ii, and his essay, 'The Crown as Corporation', in his *Collected Papers*, vol. iii, Cambridge, 1911.

W. S. Holdsworth, *A History of English Law*, vol. iv, London, 1924. [Especially the sections on English political thought in the sixteenth century. See also the same writer's *Some Lessons from our Legal History*, The Macmillan Co., New York, 1928.]

J. N. Figgis, *From Gerson to Grotius: Studies in the History of Political Thought (1414–1625)*, Cambridge, 1916, and the same writer's 'Political Thought in the XVIth Century' in *The Cambridge Modern History*, vol. iii, Cambridge, 1904.

C. H. McIlwain, *Introduction* to *The Political Works of James I*, Cambridge, Mass., 1918 (Harvard University Press).

A. F. Scott-Pearson, *Church and State, Political Aspects of Sixteenth Century Puritanism*, Cambridge, 1928.

R. G. Usher, *The Reconstruction of the English Church*, 2 vols., New York, 1910.

R. H. Tawney, *Religion and the Rise of Capitalism*, London, 1926.

For the influence of the Reformation upon the theory of natural law, see Troeltsch, and Barker's translation from Gierke (noted above); G. de Lagarde, *Recherches sur l'esprit politique de la Réforme*, Paris, 1926.

A. Lang, 'The Reformation and Natural Law', in *Calvin and the Reformation*, New York, 1909 (pp. 57–98), takes a view opposed to that of Troeltsch.

Two other important studies should be noted:

P. Vinogradoff, 'Reason and Conscience in Sixteenth-Century Jurisprudence', in his *Collected Papers*, vol. ii, Oxford, 1928.

P. Janelle, *Introduction* to *Obedience in Church and State. Three Political Tracts by Stephen Gardiner*, Cambridge, 1930.

INDEX

Acton, Lord, 81.
Albert the Great, 19.
Alexander of Hales, 114.
Allen, J. W., 4, 96, 103 ff.
Anabaptists, 106–7.
Andrewes, L., 116.
Anglicanism, 88–9, 140.
Aquinas, *see* Thomas.
Aristotle, Aristotelianism, 3, 16, 19, 22, 25–9, 31, 33–6, 49–54, 56, 65, 87, 113, 128.
Augsburg, Peace of, 82.
Augustine, St., 10, 21, 24, 28, 30, 50.
Austin, J., 61, 63.
Averroism, 48, 86.
Aylmer, J., 103–4.

Bacon, F., 123 *n.*
Bancroft, R., 105, 111 *n.*, 140.
Barker, E., 118.
Barnes, R., 100 *n.*
Bartolus of Sassoferrato, 38.
Baxter, R., 88.
Bekinsau, J., 98 *n.*
Bellarmin, Cardinal, 40.
Bernheim, E., 12.
Beza, 113.
Bilson, Th., 101 *n.*
Bodin, J., 63, 85, 132, 133, 135.
Bonaventure, St., 114.
Boniface VIII, 41, 73–4.
Bracton, 91.
Bridges, J., 111 *n.*
Browne, R., 109 *n.*
Bullinger, 104 *n.*
Burghley, 123 *n.*, 124 *n.*
Burke, 118.

Calvin, 105, 112, 113.
Canonists, canon law, 47, 93, 97, 108.
Carlyle, A. J., 13, 20, 22, 23, 32, 90, 128.
Cartwright, Th., 106, 108, 109 *n.*
Chambers, R. W., 99.
Church, R. W., 111, 117.
Cicero, 14.
Coleridge, S. T., 116.
Cooper, Th., 108 *n.*, 110 *n.*

Corpus Juris, 30.
Counter-reformation, 31.
Covel, W., 114–15.
Cranmer, G., 132.
Croce, B., 3.

Dante Alighieri, 19, 27, 37, 48, 50, 53, 73, 74, 84.
Duns Scotus, 112.

Elizabeth, 101, 103 ff., 122–3.
Erastus, Erastianism, 73, 142.

Fathers, 14.
Figgis, J. N., 4, 12, 17, 138.
Fortescue, Sir J., 40, 91.
Foxe, E., 98.

Gardiner, S., 98, 140.
Gelasius, Gelasian principle, 12, 43, 47, 73.
Gerson, 93.
Gierke, 4, 12, 17, 35, 37, 52, 55, 56, 87, 88.
Gilson, E., 87.
Gladstone, 116, 142.
Gooch, G. P., 134.
Goodman, Ch., 101 *n.*, 103 *n.*
Gough, J. W., 129–30.
Grabmann, M., 40.
Gratian, 79.
Green, T. H., 3.
Grotius, 119.

Hales, J., 116.
Hammond, H., 116.
Hegel, 18, 85.
Henry VIII, 95 ff.
Hoadly, B., 116.
Hobbes, 61, 90, 141.
Holdsworth, Sir W. S., 134, 136.
Hooker, R., 88–90, 94, 105 ff., 117–42.
Houk, R. A., 131.
Hutton, M., 124 *n.*

Janelle, P., 98.
Jewel, J., 101 *n.*